Not Really An Alaskan
Mountain Man

DOUG FINE

Alaska Northwest Books®

Anchorage • Portland

Grateful acknowledgment is given for reprint use of Page 5 excerpt by Douglas Adams,
Mostly Harmless, Random House, Inc.; Page 8 citation used by permission Merriam-
Webster's Collegiate® Dictionary, 11th Edition © 2003 by Merriam-Webster, Inc.
(www.Merriam-Webster.com); Page 17 Jack London excerpt from *To Build a Fire and
Other Stories* published by Bantam Books; Page 205 excerpt from *Jack London: Three
Novels: The Call of the Wild/White Fang/The Sea-Wolf and Forty Short Stories* by
Random House Value Publishing.

Front cover, from left: Joel Doner, Calvin Lauwers, Doug Fine, Melvin Brown, Ben
Clayton. *Back cover:* Scott Ruttum and Stormy. Mount McKinley photo © Peg Redding.
Thank you to Anchorage's Millennium Hotel for use of the moosehead!

Library of Congress Cataloging-in-Publication Data
Fine, Doug.
  Not really an Alaskan mountain man / by Doug Fine.
    p. cm.
  ISBN 0-88240-590-X (pbk.)
  1. Fine, Doug. 2. Outdoor life—Alaska—Fritz Creek Region. 3. Country life—
Alaska—Fritz Creek Region. 4. Winter—Alaska—Fritz Creek Region. 5. Log cabins—
Alaska—Fritz Creek Region. 6. Fritz Creek Region (Alaska) —Biography. 7. Fritz
Creek Region (Alaska) —Social life and customs. 8. Fritz Creek Region (Alaska) —
Social life and customs. I. Title.

  F914.F75F56 2004
  979.8'3—dc22

                           2004008769

Alaska Northwest Books®
An imprint of Graphic Arts Center Publishing Company
P.O. Box 10306, Portland, Oregon 97296-0306
503-226-2402 / www.gacpc.com

President: Charles M. Hopkins
Associate Publisher: Douglas A. Pfeiffer
Editorial Staff: Timothy W. Frew, Tricia Brown, Jean Andrews,
    Kathy Howard, Jean Bond-Slaughter
Production Staff: Richard L. Owsiany, Susan Dupere
Editor: Ellen Harkins Wheat
Cover Design: Elizabeth Watson
Interior Design: Barbara Ziller-Caritey

Printed in the United States of America

*For the cottonwood and spruce that I passed
on my runs up and down East End Road.
These trees returned to the soil in the June 1999
Fritz Creek forest fire,
at least partly so that my cabin and this book would not.
For Brenna Brown and family. Thanks for the writing haven.
And for JM, for teaching me my colors.*

When I first arrived . . . they were very nice to me and I
thought I should help them out a bit. You know,
I'm an educated chap from a high-technology culture,
I could show them a thing or two. And of course, I couldn't.
I haven't got the faintest idea, when it comes down to it,
how anything actually works. I don't mean like
video-recorders, nobody knows how to work those.
I just mean something like a pen or an artesian well or
something. Not the foggiest. I couldn't help at all.
One day I got glum and made myself a sandwich.

— Douglas Adams, *Mostly Harmless*

Contents

Introduction
Arriving in Alaska without
KNOWING HOW DO THINGS

Cheechako, n. [Chinook Jargon, 1897]: Tenderfoot.
—*Merriam-Webster's Collegiate Dictionary,* 11th Edition

This book is about switching from Big Macs to whale meat. Or, to state my intentions when I moved to rural Alaska in March of 1998, this book is about someone who wanted to feel indigenous. Indigenous is how everybody felt up until a couple of hundred years ago. That is to say, part of a physical place.

By age twenty-four, I had realized I was happiest in places where indigenousness was possible. And that meant places that are still ecologically alive. Like thousands of other people, I learned this from experiences like hiking past buffalo in Yellowstone Park and being tailed by a wolf on my first visit to Alaska. At the same time, I had learned that the amazing position modern urban society finds itself in does not provide a satisfying niche for me. Not if the air is going to be dirty and I have to spend a third of my life in a cubicle. This used to be a planet full of places that were alive. Now there are a few. Even fewer if you mainly speak English and want reliable Internet access.

I came to understand that this was largely why, despite many fine times growing up within forty miles of Manhattan—that fun city millions of people are still risking everything to reach—I had never felt at home there. I've asked around, and folks tell me that feeling at home, while important, is not such a rare condition. Billions of people evidently feel at home. Alaska, from the first moment I arrived, felt like home.

I was fortunate to realize I wanted to live someplace ecologically alive right at the time that modern society became mobile: I feel closest to transcendent when I have both a moose and a laptop within twenty yards. I didn't see a contradiction between living amidst wilderness and being a digital human. I liked that my day's plans might include both berry picking and receiving instant uncensored e-mail news about elections in Guatemala.

* * * * *

The indigenousness I craved was partly the result of something I felt was missing from my suburban upbringing. That something is Knowing How To Do Things. "Things" include skills like discerning where a water source is, killing one's own food, and knowing how to start a fire with wet wood.

These are all activities so basic to the actual Alaskan Mountain Man, they are akin to blinking. If you haven't touched intestines in the previous six months, if you've got all three joints on all ten fingers, if you haven't figured out that rubber repels water better than the expensive Space Age materials hawked in gear stores, you're not a local up here. You're a "Cheechako."

A Cheechako is perhaps best described as someone who thinks he or she wants to live in Alaska and imitate the lifestyle of the Rugged Individualist, but who isn't yet partially deaf from the sound of a 49cc chainsaw engine. Or, in everyday usage, Cheechako means inept new guy—the opposite of Mountain Man.

Where I grew up, very few people Know How To Do Things anymore. It has not been a societal goal for last few thousand years in educated Western culture, nor, by extension, is it a Darwinian selected-for trait. There was other stuff to think about in middle-class New York society, usually in the realm of pursuing postgraduate degrees and the acceptable professions: medicine and law. These pursuits generally start around nursery school, about the time I could've been learning How To Do Things. That neither of these professions really interested me garnered me something of a reputation for laziness. By the time I was out of college, I just wanted to write in a beautiful place, following a day of being at least slightly responsible for the fact that I was alive. And in truth, I can be a bit lazy (I prefer the term contemplative). I think it's good for the constitution, like a cup of green tea.

Since I came to Alaska not Knowing How To Do Things, I was, of course, a Cheechako. I accepted this. But I was willing to learn.

And before I learned that I was not exactly a whiz at Doing Things, I had visions of becoming being quite a radical neo-indigenous human. I realize now that the pleasure I take in successfully catching a salmon is no more legitimate than the alpha male satisfaction my dad feels when finding a parking spot near his Manhattan apartment: in his ecosystem, that is survival.

For me, though, it is a little bit different. I don't know why "living ecosystem" is such a high neighborhood requirement for me. I just have genes with a sense of humor, I guess: they want me in the subarctic, via a 3-million-year journey from Africa via Israel, Poland, and Long Island. With my own combination of chromosomes and experience, that's where I feel content.

I know it may sound silly, but I wanted to be content. And I envisioned contentedness in a life of tangibility, of at least beginning to Know How To Do Things. So I made the decision, in 1998, to finally move to Alaska after five visits. The problem was, I didn't have any survival skills. I couldn't "Do" anything. I don't mean I lacked the ability to build an igloo in an emergency. I mean I lacked the ability to build a doghouse with an instruction manual.

This book covers the year of rural living that either turns one into an Alaskan or causes one to leave Alaska: the first autumn and winter through the start of the second autumn. When I look back on it now, my

Introduction

first winter in Alaska represented a clear if tentative progression from a sleepwalking, preservatives-eating, TV-quoting automaton to a member of the animal kingdom who, if not yet receiving a diploma from the University of the Wild, was at least aware of the courses he still had to take.

* * * * *

And, most important, I survived. A large portion of Fritz Creek, Alaska, may still be chuckling at the various ineptitudes I displayed during that first winter. But no one can deny one key thing: I made it through alive. Some don't. I am still here in Alaska. Some aren't. And the winter of 1998–99 was one of the harshest in memory. I must've done something right.

But am I "indigenous"? Well, I guess I should further describe what I mean by this term, beyond just feeling like part of a place. On a deep, possibly chromosomal level, I think members of our species are designed to Do Things. I think this is beyond culture. In other words, I like having to work to keep my home warm and to catch dinner I think it keeps me more attuned to the deeper levels of what I am experiencing. (Although believe me, I am envious when I visit friends in Seattle and they simply flick a thermostat dial and we get toasty.) My separation from this apparently crucial genetic circuit had gone on so long, and the resulting empty space so colorfully filled with everything from the sports pages to must see TV, while growing up I was unaware that Doing Things was even a possibility. My genes knew, but they had almost forgotten.

This is why I like to think the term "indigenous" implies a remembering, more than simply being an ethnic adjective. A remembering of the way my primate genes, for better or for worse, tell me to live, which is in sync with my ecosystem. I guess I'm saying that I think indigenousness can be relearned by someone who has been pulled away from life on the planet. True, if my first year in Alaska was any indication,

I am either recessive in the primate survival gene or it's taking me a really long time to remember indigenousness.

* * * * *

If moving to Alaska for me represented the beginning of a slow awakening, what this book documents, really, is some of the wake-up calls. These chapters often tell the tale not just of the extreme adventure most of us picture when we imagine life in the Last Frontier. They reveal the little details that the most famous adventure narratives skip over.

Jack London writes of dog mushing and prospecting, for example, not of trying to brush his teeth when the pipes have frozen. In other words, the reader of these pages should prepare not only for dashing from polar bears (which actually happens), but also for mechanical problems with my snowmachine. Not just for wandering lost across a snowscape, but for praying that I had been specific enough about a pick-up time with the local water-taxi driver.

Oh, sure, I get stranded in subfreezing conditions in the middle of winter and everything, but I think such experiences are all the more harrowing because I wouldn't know how to butcher a moose even if one had died at my feet.

So even my "routine" first year contained the life-or-death components of the archetypal Far North adventure narratives. But the sources of the problems were usually down-to-earth ones: engine troubles or human misunderstandings. It's the Jack Londons, in my opinion, who recklessly left out these niggling details and lured us would-be indigenous to the polar regions unprepared for the mundane but crucial keys to survival. I suppose this was a conscious literary decision. It is uncool, from an adventurer's perspective, to complain that your feet are cold because you wore the wrong boots on the arctic pack ice. I plan to expose that myth. We Alaskans get very cold.

But even if I do expose the day-to-day realities that rural Alaskans

Introduction

need to face in order to survive, I'm sure I won't shatter the aura of legend that elevates all Alaskans to near-superhuman status at Lower 48 cocktail parties. That's because we Alaskans have perfected a method of speaking to Outsiders (and to each other) that I call Free-Range Bullshitting. You've all heard it. The exaggerated tales of brown bear encounters we tell at cocktail parties are the quintessential Free-Range stories that perpetuate Alaska legend and ensure that there is no such thing as a Cheechako to most of the world. One becomes a Mountain Man merely by the geographical decision to live in Alaska. Even with my inability to master basic rural skills, the general non-Alaskan will consider me to possess some kind of mettle merely for steering my car here. Every society needs its myths. Glad I can help.

Free-Range Bullshitting is not the same as regular bullshitting, as it generally contains the seeds of truth, uttered without filters by someone with enough bravado to paint the story just the way he or she sees it. Free Ranging is more like improv over the chord changes called the facts. Think of it as artistic embellishment. Alaskans practice it so widely because there simply aren't enough witnesses to dispute their version of the facts. It's a liberating phenomenon. I first learned Free Ranging, I now realize, the way a lion cub learns behavior among the members of its pride: from the bear tales of the people I met on my own early trips to Alaska.

But Free Ranging aside, in rural Alaska today, there's still no one to hire to do your woodcutting or snowmachine repair if you lack the financial resources to maintain a staff of assistants. And yet winter still comes. Your only recourses are friends, strangers who quickly become friends, and your own ability to learn on the spot. When I reflect on this, the fact that I have survived to this point makes me wonder how so many of the pilgrims died that first winter in Massachusetts.

I still, six years later, receive help from my friends all the time. They know I'm about two steps this side of helpless, evolutionarily speaking.

Not Really
An Alaskan
Mountain Man

It was only last winter that not once, but twice, different competent people had to come to my cabin to teach me things like soldering together the U part of water pipes and replacing spent hydropower alternators.

In fact, the longer I stay here the more I realize that the human climate in the Last Frontier resonates with me as deeply as the atmospheric one. Perhaps because of the elbow room, rural Alaskans tend to be actual individuals. If I haven't embraced every social, religious, and political philosophy I have been exposed to here, my conceptual boundaries have been stretched like the definition of "is." And I have picked up little tips along the way which I have stowed away for future use. Like the fact that toilet paper, in a pinch, can be used as emergency house insulation. It's safe to say that the mental liberation allowed by the breadth of acceptable lifestyles in Alaska has proven more valuable for me as a thinker and writer than all the travel around the world I had undertaken as a freelancer prior to moving here. Folks seem to live ideas, ideas I hadn't seen implemented on a practical, day-to-day basis anywhere else on Earth.

So along with the lessons of solitude allowed by my first five acres of Alaskan spruce forest came the reality that meetings with other creatures in Alaska, human and otherwise, are magnified. You may not like everyone you meet here (in exchange for the realness, a certain soothing politeness is sometimes lost to a sharpened poetry of directness), but they'll probably be themselves. You just can't mess with people and survive too long in these environs. I think this might be one reason why strong friendships, and quarrels, seem to solidify so quickly in the Far North. I have fewer meetings up here, but they mean more.

* * * * *

And to be sure, the long periods of solitude are valuable, too. Alaska is twice the size of Texas with fewer human residents than the New York

14

Introduction

township I grew up in. Until a 1999 forest fire thinned the sound buffer around my cabin, my closest neighbor was all but out of earshot. And I found I liked this. It matched my lifestyle. I had previously gotten into a fair amount of trouble with landlords on issues like noise and nakedness.

I sure have no complaints about a lack of "alone time." This personal space factor has positive offshoots, like being able to sing "Still Crazy After All These Years" at the top of your lungs as you split wood at 5:20 A.M. on a Thursday. And negative ones, such as writhing in unheeded agony as your split clavicle leaves you upended on your icy walkway. Not that I have any concern about this happening to me. The point is that life just becomes about you and your day, and you can't help but discover who you are. There is no one to fool. "You" seeps through.

It's fortunate that there are others willing to help me along, though, as I am still not really a Mountain Man. And yet I am still here in Alaska. Why? Part of it is being awakened by the song of thrushes rather than the honking of horns. This quiet life keeps me sane. But much of it has to do with how good it feels to learn what my friend Laura calls the Three Steps to indigenous survival in rural Alaska. The Three Steps are: (1) providing one's own heat, (2) procuring one's own food, and (3) building one's own shelter. Actually, Laura merely once pointed out that learning how to use a chainsaw didn't mean I was Grizzly Adams. When she named several of the other survival skills I don't have, I pieced together the fact that there were evidently Three basic Steps.

If you have the dough, you can easily avoid worrying about the Three Steps in rural Alaska at the dawn of the twenty-first century. But I didn't have the dough in 1998, and I didn't want to. Looking back, I think my genes are happy that I listened to them.

Other than the miserable moments of fear and cold that make me constantly debate leaving Alaska, I base my general contentedness on several factors: I don't notice days and weeks passing, I enjoy being awake no matter what the hour, and I often have a smile on my wind-scraped, splinter-embedded face. I have, indeed, discovered home. I think. It's August just now, and light for sixteen hours a day. Ask me again during some February storm.

But some of my behavior at least bespeaks true settling-in: I find myself cultivating skills like shooting accuracy and a meditative appreciation of silence, rather than the sarcasm-at-the-dinner-table and college football knowledge that seems in many places to have replaced Doing Things for the alpha primate who wishes to display dominance. I still can't really Do Things. But I am enjoying the long, slow learning process.

And let's not discount the value of the sheer natural beauty that greets me from the moment I awake each morning. Take right now. As my cabin settles into its equilibrium end-of-summer messiness and I prepare some sushi, the entire sky is aglow in a long, lazy 10:00 P.M. sunset. Two eaglets in a nearby spruce are testing their wings for their first flight.

Step One: Heat

50 degrees below zero was to him just precisely 50 degrees below
zero. That there should be anything more to it than that was a
thought that never entered his head.

As he turned to go on, he spat speculatively. There was
a sharp, explosive crackle that startled him. He spat again. And
again, in the air, before it could fall to the snow, the spittle
crackled. He knew that at 50 below spittle crackled on the snow,
but this spittle had crackled in the air. Undoubtedly it was
colder than 50 below— how much colder he did not know.

—Jack London, *To Build a Fire*

Chapter 1
Avoiding Jugular Disconnect

This Three-Steps concept dominated my life in that first Alaskan cabin. It is about having fewer, but more important inputs governing the pace of your life. I was introduced to Step One (Heat) about six months after my new gig as a travel columnist provided rent money, allowing me and my golden retriever mix, Sunny, to move to a rickety, porous cabin at Latitude 59. I was just shy of twenty-eight years old.

At first, Sunny and I couldn't believe our good fortune. We didn't yet appreciate the magnitude of the fact that I came Not Knowing How To Do Things. We hopped a ferry from Bellingham, Washington to Haines, Alaska, and then drove across the Yukon in a Subaru, finally hurtling past Anchorage and down the Kenai Peninsula to the end of the road system in Southcentral Alaska. A 4,700-mile jaunt.

Wearing an electric blue jacket composed of Space Age fibers (mislabeled "waterproof"), I enthusiastically moved into the tiny one-room cabin just inland from the Fritz Creek cliffs above Kachemak Bay, some eleven miles from the closest town of Homer. Two moose were in the front meadow as I pulled down a long, winding driveway that made the cabin invisible from the dirt road above.

I thought at first I would make an independent film from my cabin, but that didn't work out, so I had plenty of time to learn about my surroundings, with only two column deadlines per week. The movie had a telling title, though: *Migration*.

A hamlet set on a tectonic land mass so unstable it made me feel like I was getting away from earthquake danger when I visited California, Homer felt at first impression somewhere between fishing village, tourist trap, Phish show, and retirement community. The town had a nonpunctual energy that kept me constantly waiting for things like "overnight" deliveries, but it was a nice compromise between road-accessible and beautifully wild. In good weather, I was a twenty-two-minute drive from downtown Homer, which was sprawling, as homesteaders sold out and subdivided into new developments amidst the older, scrappier cabins that dotted the hills. The farther away you got from town in any direction, the more sparse the dots.

In the weeks after Sunny and I arrived, a delirious hint of spring was engorging the pea-sized buds that dangled from the alder outside my new home. The first horsetails were poking through the still substantial Fritz Creek snow like asparagus shoots. Icicles were melting into dangerous, dripping spears. I recall dancing with Sunny in almost hysterical self-congratulatory elation as the first double rainbow spread across Kachemak Bay one afternoon in late March, clearly visible from our icy but thawing deck.

Fast forward to six months later. It was not even September, and winter was coming. Palpably. I could hear it in the dry rustle of the yellowing cottonwood leaves. Gone were the nineteen-hour days and aimless hikes through fields of wildflowers that had dominated the summer. I was waking up shivering.

I remember the turning point. Stepping onto my deck one late August morning and seeing my breath, I scratched my shaggy head of retreating Einstein-vertical hair, and thought, "Okay, to not freeze to death, I need things for heat. Firewood, for instance. A stove itself." Step One. I hadn't learned the name of the concept from Laura yet. But I grasped it. I had only survived up to this point because of an expensive and inefficient electric floorboard the cabin's original owner had installed against one wall. It provided exactly the amount of heat necessary to keep my bedside water bottle slushy on subfreezing nights.

And so another Cheechako was confronted with the vast difference between living in Alaska and merely visiting. In the course of about a week. This is the difference between firing off dreamy postcards of eagles to your friends and wearing the same thermals for the ninth week in a row because you can't get your buried Subaru up the driveway to the laundromat.

When I had driven north back in March, I recognized that I might have to survive, and in fact I'd always aspired to surviving, but I imagined I'd sort of pick up survival skills and Mountain Manhood along the way. I didn't realize I'd have to start acquiring these skills right away. Or I might die.

I had never, in my twenty-eight years, fired up a chainsaw. Never even held one.

* * * * *

September's leaves were decaying three weeks later when I rifled around in my dresser drawer until I found the foam bullets I used for loud electronic concerts, and worked them into my ears. All Cheechakoness considered, I thought my first day of Doing Things was going well. Midway through it now, I had a few seconds to appreciate that a cast-iron woodstove squatted inside my cabin, and I was already on to the stuff that goes into such a stove. I was much more relaxed than I had been when I first realized winter was coming.

It was time for my first chainsaw lesson. A placebo effect of inner warmth that had flowed through my belly at this realization was interrupted by what sounded like biblical wind and rain outside. Undaunted, I fitted my yellow-tinted Smith ski goggles on my forehead as I stepped out into the Alaskan afternoon, feeling a little rugged.

That feeling lasted for about a second. My friend on the rickety deck was giving me a funny look.

"What?" I asked, shivering at the threshold of the cabin. My voice erupted a bit louder and higher pitched than I had intended. I had forgotten that I was nearly deaf from the bright yellow earplugs jutting out of my head.

20

Avoiding Jugular Disconnect

Mountain Man Roger Longhenry's mouth was formed into the unmistakable O of laughter suppression on the deck steps outside my only door. The O is what I was questioning. I hadn't done anything overly Cheechakoey since a near-fatal soldering incident late in the stove installation process nearly an hour earlier. All I had done just now was step inside to grab some gear for the chainsaw demonstration. That's what he had suggested I do. "Grab some gear."

Despite the earplugs, I could still faintly feel the vibrations of Frank Zappa guitar work emerging from the cracks in the asymmetrical door I had just "shut" behind me. The music tried to compete with the wind and stinging rain falling diagonally from the latest frontal explosion in a bruised sky. But nature was winning: the heavy air ate the digital sound waves within a foot of the door.

Faced with a soaked afternoon midway into my first Alaskan September, the remnants of my placebo effect tried to summon me back inside. But I needed to know how to work a chainsaw so that I wouldn't freeze to death when winter came.

In the sloping, spruce-dotted field I had now called home for six magical months, summer's circadian spell was breaking so rapidly I felt I could see it escaping in the steam through my lips as I looked past Roger. Out over my deck and across Kachemak Bay to the south, the jutting bulbs of the Kenai Range were already frosted. We were, in local parlance, "in for some weather."

* * * * *

Roger was still almost laughing at me.

"What?" I asked again.

"Um, look at yourself," Roger choked, behind a fog of carbon dioxide and tobacco smoke. He was surrounded by the tools we had used to affix the stove to my living quarters.

For cordiality's sake, I looked down at my right thigh area.

Not Really An Alaskan
Mountain Man

"What?" I asked a third time, a little uncertain insistence in my voice this time. I threw the acutely skeletal chainsaw instructor a shrug with my palms up as though in supplication. We had been working together all afternoon, and informality comes quickly in Alaska.

"You . . . uh, planning on hitting the slopes?" Roger sort of guffawed, rubbing his hand in a downward motion over his mouth to erase his smile.

Ah, yes. The ski goggles. They were on sitting atop a full black-knit face mask of the Subcomandante Marcos variety, and they puzzled this friend of mine, who spent pretty much all of his life doing things like throwing in woodstoves and firing up chainsaws. For him to observe my coming to this process cold at age twenty-eight must have been like Bernie Williams being forced to watch Mister Rogers face his first Roger Clemens fastball.

"Well," I said, trying to surreptitiously pocket my sissified earplugs, "The chainsaw instructions clearly say 'Always wear protective eyewear.' These (tapping the goggles) are all I have."

The complete Cheechako picture was too much for Roger. He abandoned all attempts at restraint, and hacked his pack-a-day cough in rhythm with his laugh. I stooped and kissed Sunny, who was hopping around on the deck, ready for anything. Then I accepted a sip of Homer Redknot Ale (one of several outstanding local brews) from a growler jug Roger handed me between fits of gasping. I wasn't sure alcohol and powerful machinery were such a good match, but I figured one more sip could only loosen me up. I had to fold up my face mask to get a clean sip.

"Right," Roger finally choked agreeably, and began my chainsaw lesson by starting at the beginning. After two hours spent shouting instructions to me from the roof as we smashed a stovepipe through my faux-tiled ceiling, he was starting to understand the extent of the Cheechako situation he faced.

Avoiding Jugular Disconnect

"First off, you don't want to touch the bar when the engine is running," he lectured, emphasizing this statement with a firm look and the word, "ever." He passed me the sixteen-inch Poulan chainsaw handle first, after the manner of a nurse handing a surgeon a scalpel. It was heavier than I thought it would be—lumberjacks make them look so light. Then he hopped off the deck and started into the woods, still chuckling a little. I tilted my head skyward to catch some water on my tongue and took it as a good sign that the rain seemed to have eased up a notch.

* * * * *

Chainsawing up my backyard felt, as I followed Roger into the trees, like an Alaskan rite of passage. Prior to this day, I had associated chainsaws with the kind of people whose idea of Earth Day is to clear a couple dozen environmentalists off the Earth.

But it was that time of year. As of Stove Installation and Chainsaw Initiation Day, which was circa September 19, 1998 (the longer I lived in Alaska, the more difficult it was to remember exact dates and the easier it was to think in terms of seasons), I already knew that I didn't know how to do much in my new home climate. But even I recognized that the most basic, ancient ritual up here is keeping warm. To brag about surviving your first winter in the Northland, you have to survive it. To not survive it, in an era when pretty much every convenience and machinery of automation is available in Alaska, is still possible—especially in a cabin as crumbling and poorly constructed as the one I had leased back in March—but it tends to be looked down on. I shuddered when Roger had casually told me earlier in the day that there could be two weeks per winter when I would simply not be able to get to town.

We scrunched and sloshed down into the trees like two scouts: one competent, the other obviously new to the terrain. I was still fascinated by the moment-to-moment beauty that surrounded me. This distracting love of nature is an extremely dangerous phenomenon. I would go so far as to call my susceptibility to pure trancelike bliss at my Alaskan surroundings a key part of the Cheechako disease. It's a question of ability to focus. Instead of watching my step, I found myself eyeing a three-toed woodpecker. It bonked on a bean-pole of a spruce while Roger started with his next lesson. The bird had a shocking yellow splotch on its crown, and as I watched, its mate alighted beside it. I grinned at the pair, who were otherwise engaged in hunting, gathering, and flirting.

"You also want to be aware that the bar can kickback off the tree at any moment," Roger informed me as we slid down the slope of my backyard, dense with viny groundcover. At this time of year even the most solid step had a mushy, tussocky feel under my feet. Around me, much of the scraggly brush was head-high. This growth nearly hid the two dozen or so spruce that were already downed and dry because of a bark beetle infestation. These made ideal firewood.

"OK," my mouth said. My mind, though, was nostalgic for the innocent vision of Alaska cultivated by the spring arrival. Stuff like twenty-hour days. Wildflowers. Perhaps a vote for the Greens or the Libertarians or something.

Instead, I was cold and being laughed at in daylight decidedly shorter than twenty hours. Five eerie minutes shorter per day, in fact, or three hours per month. But I shook it off. I would soon be providing my own carbon-based heat. I was Doing Things.

I tore myself away from the woodpeckers, and immediately skated on some moose milk duds while trying to catch up with Roger. After twenty yards of bushwhacking, he had picked up a net lead of fifteen yards on me. He appeared unaware of this, and I could no longer hear most of his lecture. He didn't seem to be slipping so continuously in the tangled muck of my backyard, which had been frosted that morning and was an ankle-deep bog at the moment. Until just a few weeks earlier, the five acres upon which the cabin perched were aflame with tasteful fireweed landscaping. Now the wildflowers had gone to seed, and I felt thick custards of mud (at least I hoped it was mud) oozing over the top of my habitually unlaced Vasque hiking boots.

"And be sure always to s . . . mfffl . . . ," Roger explained, in a tone of voice that sounded important. He turned to face me. " . . . before you fire her up."

At least I was picking up that chainsaws had gender. It is a crucial facet of Mountain Manhood to have the jargon down. You get laughed out of Alaska if you call a snowmachine by its Lower 48 "snowmobile" moniker.

* * * * *

About thirty downhill yards from the cabin, Roger stopped near a downed spruce. He stamped down some of the surrounding ground cover, put his hand to his forehead as an eye shade, and scanned the scene. I saw he was now leaning his impossibly thin frame against an adjacent upright tree with the familiarity that a CEO might find loopholes in the tax code. I briefly couldn't tell which was the spruce and which was Roger.

I could see he was ready to continue the chainsaw field seminar, so I quickened my pace. But when I was about five yards from catching up, an overhanging branch swiped my Subcomandante Marcos hat and the attached goggles right off my head. I watched helplessly as the dripping arm of the tree catapulted skyward and out of reach with its prize.

Burdened awkwardly with the saw, I tried one spastic retrieval jump in passing and then made the dangling gear a gift. I noticed that the rain had picked up with a vengeance, as it had been doing in twenty-minute intervals all day. I felt my hair mat down immediately; sheets of frigid water were firmly obeying Newton. I was cold.

Now at his spruce lectern as I caught up, Roger had already resumed his lecture. He was employing the Alaskan didactic professorial method—the process by which a Mountain Man or Woman will gladly explain something once, maybe twice in the case of severe Cheechakoness. But there's something in his or her barely patient older sibling tone that tells you, "After that, you're on your own."

The goal, Roger was saying, was to turn a spruce tree into a series of eighteen-inch-long "rounds." When split with a maul, these would fit into my new stove.

Roger seemed oblivious to the weather, and to my slapstick performance in even reaching the spot. His earlier mirth appeared to have faded in the realness of the outdoors, and for several minutes his instructions came quickly. They involved things like oiling, priming but not overpriming, hands being kept behind the safety shield, never taking my eyes off the target, and keeping a certain angle between chainsaw bar and target tree. I tried to make a mental checklist in my head to the mnemonic tune of "A Love Supreme."

"And more than anything else," Mountain Man told Cheechako, "make sure you have a firm foothold before you fire her up."

To rimshot that point, I tripped on a trailing raspberry vine that had embraced my flopping shoelace just as these words were out of his mouth. I nearly garroted myself on the saw bar as I fell into the mud. I sat for a long moment, feeling the moisture soak through the seat of my supposedly waterproof pants.

Roger helped me up and continued in his tobacco-ravaged voice as though nothing had happened. "Remember: what you're watching for is knots—they'll kick this bar back so fast you'll be facing jugular disconnect before you realize you're rolling down this hill without your body."

"Jugular disconnect?" I wondered. "Is this an official Mountain Man term that's bandied about in chainsaw/Libertarian circles?"

Roger picked up the saw I had dropped with the fall, made a few adjustments he didn't broadcast (perhaps he felt he had already explained them earlier when I couldn't hear), and handed it back to me. He took two steps back, lit a cigarette under the protective brim of his hat, and placed his hands upon his hips.

I tugged at the starter cord. Then I looked up innocently and spoke evenly. "Nothing happened," I informed Roger.

"Don't forget to prime her," I was instructed.

I gave a few more tugs. "Still nothing," I updated him. I wiped off my muddy butt with my free hand.

"But don't prime her too much," Roger fine-tuned.

I yanked the starter cord two or three more times, grunted masculinely, and the saw roared to life. I was suddenly making so much noise that I knew I was an Alaskan in the autumn. Before I had even lowered bar to tree, I felt I had the ability to expound loudly on shortcomings in the federal governmental machinery. I noticed my position on welfare reform hardening and gun control softening. By the time I saw Sunny bolting for cover from the terrible noise, I already had a solution for taxation: eliminate it except for road maintenance and a scaled-down defense. It felt good to be a Rugged Individualist.

With Roger nodding next to me like a driver's ed instructor, I lay the chainsaw into the dead spruce. Immediately an eerie froth gurgled forth like amber blood from the pulp flying in all directions and half-blinding me. In about a second I was through a two-foot diameter of century-old wood. So I shuffled over eighteen inches, then eighteen inches more, carving rounds until I was done with the first tree.

Then I got scared. Just clutching the revving saw in the naked air made me realize the force I was dealing with. I almost panicked, not knowing how to shut the thing down. Holding the device away from my body at arm's length, after a brief confused do-si-do in the mud, I managed to pass the still-running saw to Roger. I felt my ears torpedoing my heartbeat rhythm out into the forest. While Roger fiddled with the saw and did something to make it shut up, I smelled an oxymoronic combination of chilled autumnal freshness and rancid burnt motor oil.

I kneeled unsteadily in a mossy glen and tried to look brave as I struggled to remember exactly why I had come to Alaska.

When I had calmed my parasympathetic nervous system, I noticed Roger was flashing the kind of smile parents give to young children who have just come in from pushing a pretend lawnmower outside the kitchen window. "That went as well as can be expected," he rumbled exuberantly, punching me so that I wobbled again. "You'll figure it out. It's not rocket science."

I wasn't sure whether he meant the mechanism of the chainsaw, or Alaskan survival in general. I could feel thick droplets of sweat falling from my armpits despite the 45-degree day, and I was covered up to my shins, I noticed, in sawdust. I felt not so much the satisfaction of accomplishing a regionally crucial task, as a twang of gratefulness to still be in possession of all of my digits. I had just used a tool that sank a molten bar through 100-year-old trees with the ease that one might carve a pat of butter from a stick.

"At the end there I was trying not to amputate a limb more than cut a spruce into rounds for my winter heat," I confessed to Roger.

"Um," he said, examining what he was just now noticing was a hanging pair of ski goggles not far above his head. My cowardice wasn't getting through to him.

But if Roger felt I had passed this initial test, who was I to argue? I recalled our first meeting: it had taken him about forty minutes to recognize that I would need some assistance in order to survive my rookie Alaskan winter in a square box of a decrepit cabin. The plywood, linoleum, and corrugated metal design theory employed in my first Alaska home was not something you'll read about in either *Architectural Digest* or *Mother Earth News.*

* * * * *

I had found Roger Free Ranging at the Down East Saloon in Homer

Avoiding Jugular Disconnect

just a few weeks earlier. There was only one available stool when I shuffled in around midnight one Friday and shook off the first hint of frost. He started right in as though we met on those two stools every week. I'd say Roger spent the first half hour of our acquaintance describing the stained glass windows he was going to renovate on a cathedral in Portland for either $20,000 or $80,000. The commission varied based on where we were vis-à-vis the Redknot Ales.

He didn't not shout a single word that evening. The words themselves varied from agonizing descriptions of having his teeth pulled without Novocain (to which he was allergic), to hysterically astute observations about Alaskan gubernatorial candidates. Roger didn't care for the "redneck felon" of a Republican challenger or the "oil slut" incumbent. Like many rural Alaskans I've met, he had a particularly focused view of the world unblurred by the media filters telling us that this Earth-destroying, genocidal mess is how it's, regrettably, supposed to be. Perhaps this clarity of vision is due to the cleaner air.

Roger returned to the stained glass window gig every time a new friend entered the saloon. The story really was a masterpiece of Free-Range improvisation. In his affably strained voice, Roger never seemed the least bit aware that each retelling of the story wasn't its debut. Sometimes he accented the latest likely commission by slugging the nearest listener in the arm.

As the evening progressed, I noticed that Roger's diet consisted almost exclusively of eggs and egg byproducts. And that his shock of salt-and-pepper hair couldn't hide a boyish earnestness and optimism in his eyes. It was like his spirit wouldn't allow his age and hard living to register. A jack of all trades, which is a common profession in Southcentral Alaska, Roger was just trying to survive in a beautiful place.

* * * * *

On and on went the pleasant Free Ranging. Up and down went the commission. Down the hatch went the egg products and hops. Finally Roger took a labored breath, appraised my electric blue jacket and shaggy hair, and asked, " 'Vi seen you 'round Homer before?"

Eyes lowered, I admitted I was new in town. There is great shame in this in rural Alaska. "How long have you lived here?" is asked in the Frontier the way "Do you have stock options?" is asked in high-tech circles.

Within minutes, Roger got it into his head that I might need some help in the survival arena. I don't know what I could've done to give him that impression. In an attempt to piece it together, I'll re-create our exchange leading to his offer of assistance, in case it sheds any light on his thought process.

He was talking about water heaters with the bartender. All I did was ask Roger if he knew where the "doo-hickey" is that "lights the . . . uh . . . pilot light thing."

"This'll be your . . . first winter in Alaska then?" he hacked at me, polishing off a drink. He said "first." He meant "Cheechako." I could see his mouth fighting not to form the words, like a racist in mixed company.

"Yep," I said, wiping my lips casually on my sleeve. "But I've been out West for almost ten years."

This earned me my first opportunity to see the Mountain Man mouth formed into the O of laughter suppression. Several folks around me, in fact, together spelled out OOOOO.

"Let me know if you need a hand at your place," he growled pleasantly when he got his face under control. "Some of this cabin-repair shit you don't want to tackle alone." He seemed a reliable person to offer such advice to a fresh Cheechako. He worked in a home supply store and was, judging by the cathedral saga, breaking into the lucrative world of contracting. The guy knew Alaska and construction, at least. Based on his cocktail napkin origami, he had that crucial sense of spatial relations and he had no less than 750 keys on a key chain the size of a bowling ball.

Avoiding Jugular Disconnect

"Well, to tell you the truth," I said, when a few beers had loosened my tongue, "I've bought this cast iron woodstove, amazingly heavy thing, and I'm thinking of installing it in the south end of my cabin. You know, for heat."

All I wanted was a tip about what kind of stovepipe to buy. Three Redknots later, Roger insisted he would be at my cabin the following Tuesday at 9 A.M. In four days' time.

"We'll look at your space, sketch a plan, run to town for the parts, and throw the fucker in," he declared, wolfing a mayonnaise sandwich. Even though my cabin was eleven miles from town in the middle of the woods, Roger seemed to know exactly where it was. He waved me off when I tried to give him directions. Then he started explaining his cathedral commission to a new arrival.

This was a fellow who took big bites out of life. I knew this because he told me, "I'm a fellow who takes big bites of life," three times the first evening we met. The kindness of his offer resonated with the treatment I had always received from Alaskans during my visits. We had one more beer. The stained glass windows were grossing $60,000 when I called it a night at the Down East Saloon.

* * * * *

On Sunday, someone told me at the gas station that Roger was looking for me. Not knowing his phone number or if he had a phone, I "Bushlined" him on Monday in an attempt to confirm our appointment for the following day. The Bush Lines are the method of rural communication whereby three times a day, local radio station KBBI (AM 890) beams out messages to folks in remote areas of the Homer region who might have, for instance, an interlibrary loan book in or a car key found in a snowbank. Basically an answering machine for people without phones.

Roger proved impossible to reach via the Bush Lines. Turns out he was living at his sister-in-law's house twelve miles from my cabin, and in fact had a phone line of his own there. It took me a few days to discover this from the bartender at the Down East Saloon.

Tuesday, the day we had agreed on, passed. So did Wednesday. At noon on Friday I found myself standing around on the deck, scouring a horizon under which autumn was rather viciously making its presence felt. Scratching my head, I pondered the age-old riddle, "If a stove installation appointment is made in a forest, and no one remembers to come and help install the stove, does the installation actually occur?"

I did an Internet search for stovepipe materials. I bought a few parts. I even measured the spot for a prospective hole in the ceiling.

Roger and two friends threw up the gravel of my cabin's long driveway in a spectacular flourish at 12:30 P.M. three Saturdays later. This is appointment-keeping in accordance with a view of time known as Homer O'clock, and it was an important early exposure for me. Homer O'clock is related to String Theory, Chaos Theory, and the General Theory of Relativity, in ways too complicated to explain here. Accompanying the men was a fair quantity of Redknot Ale.

As for the actual stove installation plan, once he made it to the cabin, it became clear that Roger hadn't minced words at the Down East Saloon, no matter how many Redknots under which they were uttered. The first thing he did was sit on the 140-pound potbellied stove, which was plopped on the carpeted half of my cabin like a coffee table. He studied the tiny space from all angles. Then he made a couple of measurements and consulted the logarithmic table. Meanwhile, he offered a few asides on the fictitiousness of the Federal Reserve System now that the dollar was off the gold standard. All this took about seven efficient minutes. This is another amazing facet of Homer O'clock: once something gets done, it generally gets done right. There is just no way of knowing when this will be, as most Homer O'clock practitioners possess defective internal alarm clocks and defunct short-term memories.

Avoiding Jugular Disconnect

After Roger effortlessly sketched a multidimensional, to-scale blueprint on a scrap of newspaper, we zapped off to town for the stovepipe extensions and roof sealant and stuff. I was gratified to see he envisioned the stove sitting pretty close to the spot I had measured. The stovepipe was the tricky engineering issue. It had to rise from the stove up to eighteen inches past my corrugated metal roof, avoiding my ceiling beams in the process.

Within an hour, hammers were hammering, holes were being bashed in my roof, and we had the place generally looking more like a crime scene than a remote rural cabin. By 3:30 P.M., the stove apparatus had been hammered, soldered, and welded into place. By 3:32, his coworkers had left and Roger, Sunny, and I were enjoying a beer on the deck.

By 3:34 I was muttering about how good it was to be alive, and how lucky we were to live in Alaska. After all, with a wood-burning stove now firmly installed in my cabin, I felt my chances for survival increasing. Even during those legendary two weeks I might be snowed in, I wouldn't freeze. I appreciated this.

Lounging, feet up on the spruce railing, I said, "Sitting out here, listening to the . . . to the 'huss' of that raven's wings overhead, it really makes you feel in sync with . . . with . . . "(I was searching for some elusive word to encompass 'all encompassing'.)

Roger finished my sentence for me: "Everything."

I nodded, and Roger gave a thoughtful pull on a beer. The weather had cleared a notch, and the smell of decaying foliage settled in over us. After a minute or two of silent appreciation of the perfect beauty around us, Roger looked up at the sky and cried out, "OK, now make it rain beer!"

* * * * *

A few minutes after this unsuccessful exhortation, Roger stood up to find his cigarettes. When he returned, his face wore a serious expression.

"How're you going to get your wood?" he asked.

It was a good question. "I thought I'd save up for a few weeks, maybe buy a used chainsaw."

"You've got enough dead trees here for ten winters," he observed and then paused for a few seconds. An idea was forming in his head. "Say, why don't you borrow my chainsaw? It's in the truck."

I had seen it on our ride to town. I had even fearfully read the warning label, knowing I had chainsawing in my future. It seemed a terribly powerful thing—"49cc's," the box had said. I wasn't sure how much even a single "c" was.

"I can't do that," I exclaimed. "That thing is out-of-the-box new. You didn't buy it just to lend it to me. You've got your own wood to cut, I'm sure."

"Actually it's my sister-in-law's," he explained, dabbing out his cigarette. "I'm cleaning out her old house for her and I found it in the attic, unopened. Keep it as long as you need. I'll use it when you're done."

Standing up and stretching, he erupted in more of an exhalation than a speaking voice, "Why don't I just . . . ahhhhhh . . . borrow your Traffic tape in exchange?" Without waiting for an answer, he stomped himself and about six pounds of mud into the cabin, which shook under his feet. I counted as he took the eight steps necessary to cross its entire length to my stereo and pocketed the *John Barleycorn Must Die* album, which had been playing on infinite loop all day. He popped in a Frank Zappa CD in its stead. Which was a good choice, I felt.

"Hey Roger, thanks so much for this," I said when he returned to the deck. "You're really, you know, helping me out here."

"Hey, I know what it's like in your . . . (pause) . . . first winter."

"Just say it," I prodded, expecting the C-word. "You know it. I know it. I'm a Cheechako."

"Hey, we all started sometime."

Avoiding Jugular Disconnect

"When did you start?" I asked suspiciously.

"Two."

"Two years ago?" It sounded doubtful. But then maybe there was hope.

"Age two. They had me splitting wood before I had all my baby teeth. The first of two sets subsequently lost."

We let the ravens reflect on that for a few minutes. I made a mental note to be as helpful to new Cheechakos once I had been promoted to Mountain Man.

"One other thing," I murmured into my Redknot after a while.

"What's that?"

"I've never . . . actually . . . used a chainsaw." I felt like an adolescent forced to admit virginity.

"Well, heck," Roger bellowed, "Let's go down into the trees and I'll show you how to fire her up." This was part of the rural primate "we're-all-in-it-together" game we play here in the Far North. I like this game.

Roger lit another death stick. "Just head inside and grab some gear, and we'll start the lesson."

A moment later, however, the sky once again opened rather theatrically in a seeming downpour of rejection of Roger's suggestion; of the very idea of arming a Cheechako with a chainsaw. "Back in a minute," I said, undaunted by the Cosmos. I didn't get specific about the mask, goggles and earplugs I planned to don.

And so it was that I emerged looking like a Zapatista preparing for the Giant Slalom, facing a mouth in the shape of an O prior to my initial chainsaw demonstration. In retrospect I remember this moment of optimism as a sort of last innocence. The real problems were to come when Roger left.

Chapter 2
Cheechako Chainsaw Repair

*W*hen I look back on it now, I realize that a lot of personal embarrassment and regional uneasiness could have been avoided if I had just admitted I had broken the chainsaw right away, and asked Roger for help. But I wanted to solve the problem on my own. I thought "Figuring Things Out" was one of the routes to knowing how to Do Things. In the end, all it cost me was two nights' sleep and nearly my life. Here's what happened, as I tried to get wood to my cabin so I could survive my first Alaskan winter.

Around 4:00 P.M. on Chainsaw Initiation Day, Roger peeled out in a flurry of Alan Greenspan jokes, Traffic music, and beer fumes. Almost immediately, I armed myself with the loaner saw. Like a panicky squirrel late to the nut gathering, I was bursting to get started in the act of Doing Things. Alaska days are still long in September, and I had at least four solid hours of light left. I was so revved up with perceived pending Mountain Manhood, in fact, that I was prepared to chew several trees into rounds manually if necessary to ensure sufficient carbon for my personal winter heating needs.

I wasn't exactly sure what those needs were. I suspected I couldn't yet bank on global warming up here in the subarctic. To be safe, I wasn't going to stop until I cut enough rounds to loft a woodpile that would last practically through summer solstice. Roof high, I felt, would do the trick. This was a precaution which seemed excessive or even borderline hysterical at the time. Now, on the other side of what even old-timers say with a shudder was the nastiest winter in half a century, I see that my estimate was barely sufficient. In any event, the abject fear that had ended my recent chainsaw lesson was forgotten moments after Roger's dust settled. He had shown me how to switch off the saw. What more was there to know?

* * * * *

Without further ado, I leaped back down off the deck with a head of steam, making for the nearest dead tree. But before I had tromped twenty mushy steps into the forest, I got startled by a moose calf ruminating in the willows. It was staring at me with gumdrop eyes. It must have wandered in while I was helping Roger pack up.

I didn't see the little nougat dollop perched atop its comically long legs until I was nearly on top of it. Far more disturbing, when I was upon it, I still couldn't see its potentially skull-crushing mother. But then Sunny came through as mediator and loudly alerted me to the mom's presence and her to mine. A short snuffly waltz ensued as all species made their respective "Danger!" sounds. Then everybody calmed down, our expressions migrated from fear to acceptance, and some equilibrium resulted, the way it always does. Sunny huffed steam ecstatically from her snout, aware of her crucial diplomatic role.

In the ensuing sensual quiet of the now lightly drizzling world, I felt the slow-motion, wavering transcendence of underwater exploration.

"This is why cells divide," I thought. "This is why I'm alive."

We animals all stared at one other for perhaps ten minutes. Slowly, from what felt like very deep in my mind, a thought was trying to work itself to the forefront. I had to conduct some sort of task. A spanking new 49cc Poulan chainsaw dangled in my fingers. Ah, yes. Survival.

Sunny and I trotted like puppies down to an appropriate spruce, without incident except for an immediate and (if I may say so) graceful tumble on my part through a root booby trap. The few remaining cottonwood leaves jiggled above me as if giggling as I sat in the mud, assessing my bruises, which were minor.

37

Not Really
An Alaskan
Mountain Man

As my pants became further saturated, I ascribed my tumbles to a Clouseau-like lack of balance. This lifelong problem is associated with the cerebellum hemisphere of the brain, a region that simply doesn't function reliably for me. Perhaps, I considered, my cerebellum—also associated with spatial relations and manual dexterity—was damaged during birth. Maybe I just needed to get it in shape. Righting myself and picking up the saw, I figured I'd establish that over the course of my Alaska residency.

I squished down through the remaining twenty yards of muck, made a vain grab for my captured safety ski goggles, which were still dangling, and tried to "fire her up" beside my next tree.

I followed Roger's instructions to the letter. I checked the bar. I primed her. I topped off her gas and oil. I did almost everything to her. A quirk of technology is that there are few sounds in physics as infuriating as the chainsaw starter cord pulled to no response. It makes a noise like *huck*. This sounds like phlegm being unsuccessfully dislodged from an elderly throat behind you on a city bus.

Again and again I yanked the cord, with its weird quasi-elastic resistance, until some vague concern about "flooding her" swam across my mind.

On the live spruce limbs above me, not far from my mask and goggles, the boreal chickadees were plentiful and vocal, and seemed to be enjoying themselves. If I listened very carefully, their simultaneous warning and welcoming sounded like *Cheeeeeechako*. From many different trees their pentatonic syncopation blended, popping the air in bubbly waves.

I made the saw say *huck* a few more times for good measure. For a few minutes, the sounds of Southcentral Alaska were *Cheeeeeechako huck. Cheeeeeechako huck. Cheeeeeechako huck.* My arm was getting tired.

Finally I concluded that there must be something wrong with the saw. This frustrated me no end, and my mood shifted abruptly. I experienced great pangs of self-pity over all the extra work I would have to do to produce my winter firewood. I felt powerful disdain for the saw and its manufacturer, and I was even a little resentful of Roger's sister-in-law for buying such a lame product. Plus, the next hammerhead front had settled in like a towel tossed over a lamp, and I was getting wetter through my hopelessly ineffective Space Age fibers. I angrily removed the spongy jacket, and tied it around my waist. I hadn't yet learned that locals favor good ol'-fashioned rubber gear. Life was so very far from the fantasy I had been living during the summer. Life, in fact, sucked.

I couldn't believe how long this darn survival was taking. Almost a day already. I had no option but to call Roger. Maybe there was some function to perform or magic word to utter in order to spark the dysfunctional device. Perhaps this had been transmitted when Roger was out of earshot as I was struggling down the meadow slope and slip-sliding on moose scat. I had been paying less than total attention during the woodpecker portion of the demonstration as well.

Back to the cabin I stomped. It took me a few grumpy minutes to work my way uphill past the moose, to whom I offered a self-conscious wave.

By the time Chainsaw Initiation Day actually occurred, I had acquired Roger's phone number. Roger answered on about the thirteenth ring.

"Did I tell you about this cathedral job I've got lined up in Portland?" he asked when he heard it was me. "Stained glass, my boy. It's the future."

I found this subject matter troubling. I was kind of hoping he'd say something like, "How's it going with the saw? Any questions?" I could hear the strains of Traffic playing in the background.

If you're going to fight the short-term memory issues in the Alaskan Mountain Man, you're never going to get anything done. You have to go with it. "That sounds great," I answered. "Will the Pope pay your travel?"

I discovered that the commission index was down slightly on open trading, to $49,000. Plus travel expenses. Then I listened to some of Roger's concerns about NAFTA.

Finally I squeezed in, as casually as possible, "So on this chainsaw rig. I primed her, oiled her, did everything just like you said, and well . . . nothing. The starter cord just makes sort of a hollow *huck* sound."

"Did you turn her on?" my chainsaw instructor asked.

And so back down into the forest I tramped, tripping past the moose and taking the abuse of the chickadees. I saw through the slanting rain needles that the moose cow had a distinctive bare patch on her right flank, probably from a bear attack or a barbed-wire fence. It looked like Groucho Marx's profile.

* * * * *

By the time I made it back to the prospective spruce, it was dawning on me that I would have to work for Mountain Manhood. Another fantasy dissolved. Tricky complications like mending fishing nets and knowing to turn on the chainsaw before pull-starting it were sure to keep popping up. Switching hands with the saw and planting my feet carefully, I remember reflecting that much has been made of efficiency since things like electricity and the internal combustion engine became widely available. No doubt more wood can be cut with a 49cc chainsaw than with a handsaw. But I briefly wondered whether, for Cheechakos, such technologies really make things easier, psychically, than the more conventional manual tools that have been used to, say, fell trees, for most of *Homo sapiens*' existence. The ones that don't require consulting prior to use.

I went through the priming routine again, and on my fourth huck, I again became responsible for the terrible sound unique to the naked gasoline-powered saw. It sent the Sunny-and-moose powwow scatter-

Cheechako Chainsaw Repair

ing as though Armageddon itself had arrived. I only remembered at this moment that my earplugs had been in my pocket all day. I imagined that my contribution to humankind might be the development of a muffler for the chainsaw. It seemed incredible, or maybe intentional, that no one had done this.

After a few minutes, though, I found myself in the swing of things. Once again I was treated to the amazing phenomenon of just how quickly a 49cc crutch can make a fellow cocky.

"I can do this," I thought scoffingly. "My Cheechako days are numbered."

Chainsaws are deceptive this way. When the wood grain is amenable, you feel like the king of all fiber. This helps explain the absence of forests after the first hundred years of chainsaws.

I spent nearly forty minutes shredding two downed 120-foot-spruce into gnome chairs. When the first spruce dotted the forest floor around me in a perforated line, I felt a surge of gratitude for these trees that had given their lives to sustain first 14 million beetles and then me. I paused for a moment to give this appreciation the emphasis it deserved. Then I sank the bar in again, savagely. My unlaced boot was wedged under a rock, my cheeks burned, and the forest air around me was speckled with fragrant suspended sawdust particles.

I was nearing the end of the second spruce when the delusions of grandeur started kicking in. "Maybe I can carve my entire winter wood supply tonight," I aggrandized.

As if to editorialize on that strategy, the chainsaw bar at that moment shot back like a razor-sharp pendulum on speed. It did this along an axis that ran a solid two millimeters wide of my right ear. It had evidently boomeranged off an impenetrable softball-sized knot. The motion actually gave me a slightly layered haircut. What happened is, as Roger warned, called "kickback." It kills people. All the time. Everything went down so fast. I barely had time to reflect that, "This saw isn't working anymore" before my head nearly filed for divorce from my torso.

My body, reacting as fast as the nervous system felt it was capable (and far too slowly), arched back, and I dropped the saw in terror in a nearby pile of bear scat. It continued to cycle for a second or two like the proverbial decapitated chicken, chopping up a moss mound and sending ursine defecation onto my chest in a paisley pattern. Embarrassed at its slow reaction to the saw's assault, my spinal cord tried to compensate now by turning my legs into the gooey material inside Stretch Armstrong dolls.

Everybody who has faced this kind of near-death has his or her own way of dealing with it. Mine was to sort of hop around guiltily to see whether there were any witnesses to the event, and then to give thanks both for Alaska's low population density and for still having a noggin that could send such insecure signals to its body. I was still alive. Steam escaped from my mouth and mixed with foul smoke as I emitted a relieved, "Hoo hoo ho ho holy shit!" Searching for the off-switch, I danced in little nervous circles around the still-humming saw.

That task completed, I remembered with nostalgia the moment when my only problem was that the saw wouldn't start. Now my life was at stake. It was as though every moment in Fritz Creek were out to prove how good I had it a moment ago. I shivered at the logic: would I soon come to think that things were actually pretty good right now? Yes.

I think in retrospect what happened next was my biggest mistake of the day, and evidence that the essence (and danger) of Cheechakoness lies in decision-making as much as wrongful action. Instead of cutting my losses there in the last light, so to speak, and breaking for a full investigation of the now-smoking saw in the morning, I thought the Mountain Manly thing to do was to "climb back on the horse" and keep going. After all, I had learned an important lesson: look out for knots. Along with "no garroting," and "turn the saw on before use," "avoid decapitation" seemed pretty much the whole story.

Cheechako Chainsaw Repair

And so, as soon as blood started flowing to my rubbery knees again, I snatched up the saw, topped off her oil, and resumed the cacophony until I was within ten feet of the end of the second spruce. My confidence was back. I chose not to notice that the smoke coming out the saw had now fully enveloped me. A fine day's work it would be. I'd split a round or two with my maul back on the deck, collect some kindling, enjoy my first fire.

Suddenly, with maybe three thin tippy-top rounds to go on the second tree, I smelled an even more sickly kind of burning than the terrifying chainsaw engine usually emitted. It was something akin to the scent of car brakes after a 6,000-foot descent. The noise was unbelievable, too— like the saw was begging for mercy. Thinking I was learning from experience like a good primate, I pulled the bar back from the tree at this irrefutable sign of trouble. This was wise, but I neglected to release the trigger. As I watched stupidly, the chain started whirling freely in a hula hoop motion and then sailed like a field goal attempt over my shoulder, through some branches, and deep into the woods. About two seconds later I heard a muffled *mumPP* somewhere behind me where the chain became a necklace around a nearby cottonwood limb.

I turned to face the direction of the launch, like a pitcher who has just served up a home run. And I switched off the saw.

Cheeeeeechako, called the chickadees.

I fetched the projectile chain, which, I was comfortably certain, was supposed to stay attached to the saw proper. It was also, I couldn't help noticing as soon as I grabbed it, extremely hot. I carried it back on a stick, like a dead snake.

How Good I Had it a Moment Ago Syndrome should be studied as a legitimate philosophy. Its ramifications were snowballing on me.

∗ ∗ ∗ ∗ ∗

Indeed, it wasn't a victory journey back up to the cabin. I trudged, heedless of balance issues and wildlife encounters, and burdened with both a chainsaw and its exiled chain-on-a-stick. Sunny looked up at me with a concerned expression.

"Uggh," I explained to her. "Even I know this isn't supposed to happen with a saw so spanking new. I only had the thing for an hour and a half." Here Roger was, in a very real way, trying to save my life with that loaner. He was the first person to really reach out to me in the Last Frontier. How was I repaying this act of kindness? By busting the thing. And nearly busting myself in the process.

As I waded toward the deck, I dejectedly almost wished I had been injured in the kickback incident, preferably superficially. Then, when I presented him with a some-assembly-required pile of parts, announcing I had launched his sister-in-law's chain into the stratosphere, Roger might feel some superseding guilt about leaving a helpless Cheechako with a loaded chainsaw.

No, of course I couldn't give him the saw in this state. But replacing it would break me. These things cost hundreds of dollars new. It was looking like a credit card nightmare—just what an almost-starving writer needs. I couldn't even face the prospect of getting him in trouble with his sister-in-law.

Schluurk schluurk schluurk said my boots remorsefully in the chilly muck of the forest as these thoughts ran through my mind.

The situation as it stood at 5:15 P.M. on Chainsaw Initiation Day also raised troubling Cheechako implications surrounding my first Doing Things performance. I was still trembling from my brush with beheading, and wasn't sure to what degree I should look at the events of the late afternoon as some sort of larger message. It didn't help that I caught a glimpse of myself in the huge bay window overlooking the deck when I neared the cabin.

I usually loved that window. It was a shuffleboard court of fly-spotted glass that comprised most of the deckside, south-facing front of my cabin. It gave a vista through my meadow and the spruce forest, and over the fierce aquamarine of Kachemak Bay to the glaciated peaks beyond. I can't count the hours I had lost just trancing on the view through the bay window.

But in it this afternoon, I saw a muddy Cheechako clutching a bundle of steaming oily metal. His hair was covered in a dandruff of sawdust, and he was shivering as he gazed back at me rather forlornly. He looked, in fact, as though he might be dreaming of a hot shower. An absurdly inadequate electric blue jacket was tied around his waist, and it was dripping rainwater like a leaky faucet. The poor guy, if our description is to be complete, was splattered with brown stuff and appeared as if he might smell of some animal's fresh defecation. I would call this fellow about as Darwinianly exposed in rural Alaska as a newborn seal in a shark tank.

"Maybe we should just pack it in," I said to Sunny, who was wagging her tail in expectation of a treat. All signs seemed to be pointing that way. With my knuckles in my mouth to soothe the bar burn, I stepped away from the disturbing image and considered my options. It didn't suit my personality, firing up chainsaws and risking decapitation, when technically there was a society down south where you just switched on the thermostat. Plus, I am a tree pacifist. I don't enjoy hacking up even dead ones. I like trees.

In retrospect, my transition from exuberance to surrender seems abrupt even to me. But near-death-by-stupidity will do that to a fellow. I was still recovering from the shock of being alive.

"How am I going to be an indigenous human?" I asked Sunny, who seemed to have no trouble adjusting. "I can't even use the amenities that make life easier."

I started rationalizing. I wouldn't be the only one to abandon an attempt at the neo-Rugged Individualist lifestyle. You can't drive ten miles along the road toward town without noticing the aesthetic decrepitude of imploded greenhouses and dilapidated cabins still redolent with ambition and good intentions. Some of these structures on close examination appear to have been vacated in a hurry.

It was in this fragile state of mind that I crossed the cabin threshold, mushed a security-deposit-draining amount of mud into the carpet, and realized I couldn't bring myself to call Roger again. Not so soon. But I needed some advice, or maybe consolation. So instead I got on the horn and called JM, who was working at the flower shop in town.

JM was a pretty Mountain Woman who for some reason had been popping over all summer. She was soft-spoken and had good posture, intelligent eyes, and an air of having passed through an intellectual feminism period. I didn't give her all the details of the day. I sort of calmly sketched for her that I had found myself obsessed with wood heat once I got the stove, and there had been some "complications."

"Why are you yelling like that?" she asked.

"Oh, sorry. Chainsaw deafness."

Then I lowered my voice and admitted cryptically, "I'm worried about the whole winter survival situation." This was no Free-Ranging semi-truth. "If it keeps up like this, I won't get anything else done, and the way things are going, I still might not survive."

"Don't sweat it," JM said, and I could tell her mouth was formed into a little O. "You're just nesting."

A few words that paint the whole picture. This was typical JM. She had five winters in Alaska to my none, and antifreeze for blood. She sprinted like a deer, knew how to tie knots, and could do crossword puzzles. All crucial Alaskan survival traits. So if JM said my behavior was normal, I wasn't going to question it.

"I'll never look at nut-gathering squirrels the same way again," I said, trying to sound lighthearted.

Still, JM didn't seem to grasp the depth of what had happened in Fritz Creek this day. I considered getting more explicit. But before I could fill her in on the discombobulated borrowed chainsaw, she changed the subject.

"Would you like to get together Monday night?" She sounded as though she had some secret in mind. "I get off at 6. Maybe you'll have resolved your . . . ah . . . complications by then."

"But . . . " I said. I wanted to unload. To confess my Cheechakoness.

"I'll come over to your place," she cut in. "I have to go. There are customers."

* * * * *

I hung up the phone and absentmindedly gave the still-frenetic Sunny a peanut butter biscuit as reward for her defense of the cabin. Maybe JM was right. Maybe I shouldn't sweat it. What she was tersely explaining with the nesting comment, I thought, was that ours is the same seasonal awareness that causes trees to know to drop leaves. In other words, I had no choice: I had to obsess over heat. Either that or go crazy thinking I was unprepared for the winter to come. And in this process, as in all aspects of life, "complications" happen. The key is to resolve them. That's what she seemed to be suggesting.

I spent a dusky half hour thinking this over, pacing around the trashed cabin to the point that I made Sunny dizzy. So she leapt on the bed to complete her daily mission of soaking the comforter. I realize now I was engaged in the important act of forgetting how close the revving chain came to my jugular. Our memories are great this way: trauma goes away like Milli Vanilli.

During this time, the chainsaw sat like an out-of-favor child's toy on the kitchen floor, still emitting heat, I noticed. I didn't want to keep it outside, lest it get below freezing. That couldn't be good, right? The device was full of potential energy, I felt, even as the chain drooped along the linoleum next to it like a mangled bicycle component. I gave it some space whenever I walked in that part of the cabin.

Not Really An Alaskan
Mountain Man

Finally, as a charcoal-and-lipstick sunset spread across the suddenly and mockingly clear sky, I looked at the saw and made a simple invocation over it. "I will fix you," I told it.

And much more was resolved in that invocation. I made a decision then and there to emerge from Cheechakohood. Or die trying. I would not leave Alaska. My arms made a conjuring motion and Sunny raised an eyebrow from the bed. In the vision that followed, I saw myself in a series of postures, as evolution textbooks show humans emerging from *Australopithecus* through Neanderthal to *Homo sapiens*. First I would proudly present Roger with a functional saw and a smile, as though nothing had happened. Then I would wrestle a polar bear into a half nelson in defense of a child in its clutches, and then I would climb Denali, in shorts. I have been told I function best in the haze of fantasy.

I started planning the chainsaw repair right away. The first thing I needed, I realized, was some time. Mountain Men aren't built in a day. So I initiated a cover-up on a scale of which James Carville would be proud. I would screen for Roger's calls, mostly invitations to beer, and tell no one about the chain dismantling. I learned early on that word spreads fast in Homer. When I dropped my car key in a twelve-foot snowbank the week I arrived, clusters of people were laughing about it in the laundromat the next day. I figured it was reasonable for me to keep the saw for about three to five days.

I had other motivations for buying time, as well, besides doing right by Roger's friendship. Practically speaking, I still had a lot more wood to cut into rounds to even approach what I estimated to be a winter supply—probably six or eight more trees worth. There were plenty to choose from: at least twenty-five mature spruce down within view of the deck. It would take a day and a half with a functioning chainsaw.

"Where to begin, where to begin?" I wondered, gently fingering the chainsaw's gears and familiarizing myself with its inner structure. I found myself kneeling over the device with a rag tucked into my shirt

Cheechako Chainsaw Repair

like a bib. I had pulled off the engine's green plastic casing for the exploratory surgery. I made a lot of hmmm sounds.

Then it came to me: I'd seen someone unscrew a chain bar on a TV home repair show once, and, as it had looked simple to reattach, I now gingerly picked up the device, and did this. So far so good, although now I had three parts to deal with: the base of the saw, the bar, and the chain. Right on the kitchen floor, I cleared away clumps of coagulated grease and sawdust from the bar, and then threaded the chain back onto it. Then I re-screwed the bar to the saw base. Easy enough. Fifteen minutes total. What was all this worry about? I brought the thing outside to the deck, added some oil, primed her, switched her on, and fired her up.

Before Sunny could leap for cover under the bed, the chain drooped off like melting ice cream from a popsicle stick.

I unscrewed and cleaned and re-screwed the bar again, and fired her up. The chain immediately bailed again. It looked like a frown as it hung limply from the bar.

I repeated this process several more times.

There was something I was missing. The act of starting the engine caused the chain, which seemed as tightly wound as Ralph Nader discussing real wages, to instantly forget that I had threaded it securely to the bar. It ignored the principle of centripetal motion.

But I was emboldened now, as the chainsaw repair thus far hadn't reduced my number of limbs or anything like that. I redoubled my dedication to fixing this thing. I was not going to remain a Cheechako forever. I started with a call to Homer Saw and Cycle, which seemed the appropriate shop in town—it had a large selection of chainsaws, in any event. Amazingly, they were still open. I managed not to give my name. The woman who answered had good diction. She asked me, "What initially went wrong?"

"The chain just sailed off like a hula hoop—almost took my head off. Is that normal?"

Pause. "That happens," she said reassuringly.

"So I didn't necessarily break the saw?" I asked hopefully.

"Not necessarily," she agreed. "It's not that usual for a new saw to, ah, eject its chain, though. What were you cutting, a rock?"

She walked me through a complicated series of instructions centered around maintaining leverage on the bar while tightening the screws so that the chain stayed fast. I thanked her and implemented the maneuvers. More chain droop. Spirit droop, too.

"Forget Mountain Manhood," I thought as the evening settled in. "That is never going to happen." I accepted this. Cheechakohood was a reality that might just be another inevitable offshoot of cerebellum disability. I would try to bravely survive with that handicap. My worries had moved on. I was now beginning to get very nervous that I truly had done considerable damage to the saw. I kept picturing a decade-long Visa balance if I needed to replace the thing. Could a mere knot have launched the terrible machine toward higgledy-piggledy? Weren't knots part of tree-cutting life?

What a day. I was exhausted, and probably not the most attuned playmate for Sunny that night when we took our usual walk-and-wrestle after a halibut dinner. Nor did I sleep much on that shameful Initiation Day evening, despite a soothing raindrop rhythm ting-tocking on the roof. I had felt too guilt-ridden even to light my inaugural fire in the stove. The potbellied receptacle seemed to stare at me sarcastically, and actually radiated coldness into the cabin. Wind whistled in through the stove pipe we had worked so hard to install.

I woke up desperate, confused, and disappointed that the scary events of the previous day hadn't been a bizarre dream. There was nothing to do but continue with the Cheechako Chainsaw Repair. I spent the morning pulling apart and reassembling the 49cc shredder. My life was like the film *Groundhog Day*: the result was always the same. The chain seemed to have adopted a pro-environment policy.

Cheechako Chainsaw Repair

* * * * *

Something was wrong with the saw. Was it something internal? I shut off the engine for the final time. "It is time," I sighed as the miraculous silence returned like a kiss upside the head, "to confess." I heard a woodpecker bonking, and the thought, "All quiet on the Cheechako front" crossed my mind. I felt I understood the moment after the Independent Council's report is irrevocably published.

I called Roger and hinted that I needed some tips on the saw. He updated me on the cathedral job and invited me over for egg products the following day. I still didn't feel as though I deserved a fire in the stove that night. I slept one more cold sleep in the cabin. Sunny didn't mind, the insulated beast. But it required a great act of courage for me to emerge from my comforter onto the frozen floor that Monday morning.

I carried the saw up to Roger's porch under an afternoon drizzle, along with a refilled container of gasoline and a can of oil. He opened the door, rubbing his eyes. It was only 1:00 P.M., and he hadn't yet had breakfast's three servings of eggs and fried lipids.

"Got a winter worth o' rounds?" he asked.

"Er, not exactly . . . ." I fessed up with head bowed. I left out nothing. The failure to watch out for kickback. The airborne chain. I even told him about not paying attention to the safety lecture back when the woodpeckers had caught my eye. "This chain just won't stay reattached," I concluded. "I don't know what I did to her."

Roger yawned, took the saw, examined it for about a third of a second, and with a dismissing wave told me there was nothing wrong with the saw itself. "This isn't the right chain for this saw," he said. "See how it's stretched? That chain should never have been bought for this saw."

We made a run to town, returned with the right chain, and it took about four minutes to assemble the saw. Maybe less. I found this hard to reconcile, given my futile forty-eight-hour battle with the disabled implement. Here I was discovering another key difference between the Cheechako and the Mountain Man mind. A priceless chasm of know-how.

"You're on your way," Roger said, sending me back to the forest following egg-salad sandwiches with extra mayonnaise and a Bailey's chaser.

* * * * *

That evening found me naked, melting from an excessive inaugural spruce fire that had Sunny curled in a carbon monoxide coma on the bed. The fire also sent its flames licking through the stove's carelessly half-closed hatch, nearly torching the cabin after some of my Space Age fibers ignited where they had been hanging too close.

When that crisis was dealt with in the nick of time by the saturation of half the cabin with madly thrown buckets of water and mud, I sat myself at the laptop, trying to piece together a column. Stymied, I stepped out onto the deck in my birthday suit for a deep lungful of cool air. While the radio, on cue, belted out Etta James singing "At Last" through the cracks in the cabin, I saw them, grooving in the slate dusky light: the Groucho cow and her calf. Few species are not drawn to Etta. I sighed, as if for the first time in a long time, emitting a sound akin to, "Everything's going to be all right."

Having received a narrative booster shot from that encounter, I hopped back on the keyboard. My column wound up being about the importance of making friends while traveling. I almost certainly would have dwelled even longer on the friendship theme had I known that within nine months, Roger Longhenry would be gone from Alaska for treatment of a heart condition that seemed to surprise no one but me. But I didn't know that, and felt only gratefulness for his general good energy. They say there is a shortage of this in the world of late.

A cup of miso steamed at my bare arm, and Billie Holiday was lamenting unhealthy relationships on the box. I finished typing a sentence and looked down from my chair. I noticed that sawdust shavings still filled my boots. I smiled at myself in the bay window. Then I focused back on the screen.

Either five or five hundred minutes later, I heard a soft knuckle tap on the bay window. I looked up to see a be-mittened JM. She was almost totally concealed by the geyser of steam swirling from what appeared to be a bursting pie in her arms. But between wisps I could periodically make out the little O into which her mouth was formed. This was possibly caused by the fact that I was sitting at my keyboard nude in an Alaskan cabin well after the first frost.

"You've got guests," she said, when I grabbed a towel and opened the door, nearly knocking her backward with a back draft of sauna-level heat. "I scared them with my headlights."

"My guard moose," I explained. "They protect me from the bears."

She tamped off her boots on the welcome mat and passed me the pie. Her tight dark ringlets peeked out from her hat.

"You're not the only one rumbling through the seasonal motions and their . . . complications," she revealed, waving away a wall of spruce smoke from in front of her face. "I've been suffering from compulsive berry-picking. And I can't seem to stop baking. (Pause.) Whoo. What smells?"

"Oh, sorry, jacket burning," I disclosed as we gave ourselves raspberry mustaches. Then I clarified, "Complications."

* * * * *

This conversation was the beginning of what turned out to be a great date. At one point JM exclaimed, "Oh! I forgot something," and scampered over to her jacket. She returned holding a black Subcomandante Marcos knit hat, encircled by a pair of ski goggles.

"These yours?" she asked. "I found them in the mud off the deck."

I guess I was still smiling inside when I stopped in at the Fritz

Not Really
An Alaskan
Mountain Man

Creek General Store the following morning. Laura, the lithe and sardonic daytime employee there, is a friend of mine. Our friendship consisted primarily of her teasing me about my Cheechakoness. As the wooden edifice of the General Store was my principal source of nutrition, videos, fossil fuels, and headlines, we cultivated this relationship frequently. On this day, she took one look at my stove-warmed face and said, "You're looking chipper. Is that a burn on your jacket? Something's up, isn't it?"

As such inquiries are typically genuine in rural cultures, I Free Ranged the entire Chainsaw Haircut and Repair saga right at the counter, focusing on the danger to myself and my ultimate triumph. Continuing my pattern of failing to learn humility from experience, I had, with one stove fire, started to get a little proud of myself again. I felt my winter heating worries disposed of and my Cheechako days numbered. I leaned my elbows on the counter and smiled at Laura unctuously, as if to convey, "Pretty impressive, huh?"

That was when Laura started terrorizing me. The twenty-year-old Mountain Woman absorbed my tale straight-faced, and then, in her old-soul Gertrude Stein deadpan, said, "Step One."

She then paused, mimicking my pose at the counter until we were nose-to-nose, as though her two words said it all. They didn't, so she elaborated. "You have dispatched with the simple, mindless task of cutting rounds with a chainsaw. Nice work. Ever have to sleep outside in the winter time? Ever hunt a meal?"

This was the first time I had heard about the Three Survival Steps, in so many words. I felt it summed things up nicely. Or I should say it instantly frightened me back into my Vasque boots and Marcos hat. It reminded me I was just beginning to understand the concept of Doing Things as the first kiss of winter steamed my breath, turned Sunny's whiskers into mini icicles on our runs up East End Road, and forced me to buy a scraper to handle the morning frost designs on my windshield.

Cheechako Chainsaw Repair

This was the first, simplest Step One task I had so tenuously accomplished with the resolution of Chainsawgate. If I were ever to build a cabin of my own, I'd have to learn Things like digging a well, planning a septic system, attaching a roof, plumbing a sink, wiring electricity, and connecting telecommunications with the nearest satellite. All of these activities except maybe the last one are second nature for a Roger Longhenry; akin to blinking. I was years away from tackling these tasks myself. And even with a stove and firewood, I would soon learn that my cabin would technically be an igloo by 3:00 every morning all winter long, or whenever twenty minutes had passed since my last fire went to embers.

Before I left the General Store, Laura gave me amnesty on a movie rental late fine in exchange for the meek look on my face. I had never been a local before. I relished the special treatment. When I shuffled away she was hauling cases of beer to the impressive General Store cooler. If Fritz Creek were cut off from the rest of the world, the General Store would continue to supply alcohol for weeks.

Despite Laura's ribbing, or thanks to it, I felt that I at this point in September nourished a balanced perspective. "From here," I told myself as I returned to the Subaru with my mail, some insulation tape, and a maul-handle repair kit, "there is no turning back."

I was sure Alaska had been the right decision. Thanks to the kindness and humor of a few animals, human and nonhuman, I floated through the remainder of that first autumn in some kind of overall nesting high. The golden-tinged woods were ready for their insulating blanket, and so, I imagined, was I.

Chapter 3
Re-Re-Confirming
the Water Taxi

The two and a half months after the resolution of the Chainsaw Incident went so well inside the cabin that I started getting ideas that I should know how to survive outside it. It seemed the next logical phase in my Step One exploration. Or maybe I was trying to respond to Laura's challenge. As the shortest day I had ever experienced approached, I aspired to be the kind of guy who looks out over an Alaska frostscape and sees a giant playground. The Alaskan Mountain Man, I fantasized, was not just willing to trek into the heart of winter, to ignore the snow accumulations (which of late had averaged something like seven inches per day in Fritz Creek), and to sleep in the icy wilderness. He was prepared to enjoy it. This was the stuff I read about in Jack London stories.

For one night at least. No need to overdo it the first time out.

I had thought this over rather hypothetically all autumn from my wood-chopping block beside the deck, as I squinted out over the icy griddle of Kachemak Bay. What I was looking toward was simply my favorite spot on Earth. It was a secluded little pond, polished turquoise by sunlight and the Grewingk Glacier, which fed it. I had discovered it back in July on a backcountry trek, and had visited it several times during the summer. Sometimes I liked just hiking to it and splaying myself out along its banks, preferably with my djimbe drum. I always returned to the cabin rejuvenated. And the pond without fail visited my dreams as a symbol of renewal, like a fountain of psychic youth.

The seductive liquid hourglass was too far away to see from my deck, nestled as it was in the forest about three miles up a trail from the far shore of the bay. But it was due southeast, almost directly across from my door. So each day as I split my rounds, I bestowed on myself a kind of wilderness X-ray vision and imagined myself romping around the pond's lichen-covered cliffs.

As October turned into November and Fritz Creek took on a solid-state glaze, I started wondering vaguely what the pond's winter color would be like. Emerald, I imagined. Maybe shimmering jade: trapped molecules of 20,000-year-old water, frozen at their moment of birth. Perfect for ice skating.

Right through Thanksgiving my fantasizing stayed firmly in the realm of the theoretical. You don't cross Kachemak Bay at this time of year unless you have to. The waves are too big. I could see with my own eyes the daily sermon of apocalyptic nastiness the bay shot skyward in loping geysers. But a fellow can ponder.

I had pondering time in surplus. I spent these post-Chainsawgate months getting to know JM better, innertubing with Sunny in the woods, and, most of all, building my multistoried woodpile, whose rumbling adjustments were a constant demonstration of chaos theory.

I chopped wood for two hours a day off the deck with a heavy hickory-handled ax whose iron maul was prone to flying off. No matter how cold the morning, the coming of light would find me hacking away at my spruce and whistling to the tune of "Thank God I'm a Country Boy." Sunny would then usually let off with a censorious howl.

And so went October and November. It was a peaceful time of settling in and "nesting," of column-writing and of face-melting stove fires. JM would sometimes swing by with her sketchbook in the evenings and we'd sip tea while I advised readers why they could ignore State Department travel advisories, or how to get cheap last-minute bookings on Galapagos cruises. My eyes were perpetually red from my nonairtight stove. I didn't mind.

✳ ✳ ✳ ✳ ✳

This serene period lasted until one evening in early December, the third I think it was, when I heard the trucker with the Relaxed Tone. He plopped himself and about five pounds of beard down on a stool next to Roger and me at the Down East Saloon. Then he started talking.

The trucker had experienced a rough evening a few days earlier. He had almost frozen ("to death," needless to say) during a breakdown in a remote area near Fairbanks. With the lubricant of several beers, he described his experience being trapped batteryless for a long, dark night in a 50-below whiteout. He called the incident "outside my Comfort Zone."

The key component of this harrowing and convincing Free-Range tale, as far as I was concerned, was that the trucker delivered the "Comfort Zone" line in this particular, almost distracted, ultimately Relaxed Tone. It was the ho-hum vocal timbre with which one might observe, "The 49ers are pretty good this year." The impact of the tale was only slightly softened by the bartender, who had heard this kind of epic for decades. She kept her eyes on the tap until the trucker finished the whole drawn-out story, topped off a Redknot, and then said in a pretty Relaxed Tone herself, "My Comfort Zone is you paying off your tab."

I left the saloon that night wanting to have a story to relate in a Relaxed Tone. Every Alaskan Mountain Person remembers and Free-Ranges his or her first, usually accidental, winter night spent sleeping outside, exposed in the wilderness. Disguised hubris is apparently part of the Cheechako-shedding process. First you garner a legitimately harrowing survival story. Then, with the vocal quality you assume during this special kind of Free-Ranging, you indicate that things like whiteouts, typhoons, avalanches, bear attacks, and frostbite are fun. Such occurrences might not explicitly be the goal, but the implication is that you're Not Really An Alaskan Mountain Man if you haven't experienced them.

Re-Re-Confirming the Water Taxi

"My chainsaw kicked back" just didn't make the cut as a Free-Range saga. Everyone at the Down East Saloon was in agreement on this.

I drifted into innocent sleep December 3 without realizing that the trucker played right into the hands of whatever force had been trying to get me to that pond all autumn. Prior to that Comfort Zone catalyst, I had just been awash in loosely formed Step One fantasies.

And so, up with a candy-striped sunrise the following morning at the crack of 10:30 A.M., I gaped across the bay and made the definitive decision: I was going to visit the pond. Skate on it. Camp beside it. Achieve Mountain Manhood. It was a resolution that would have seemed patently unrealistic to me a week earlier, but somehow on this flurrying morning, it felt absolutely right.

Getting to this pond was simply a one-hour matter of crossing the steaming winter cauldron of Kachemak Bay—of skipping across what of late had been some of the hairiest and most unpredictable waters I had ever seen. I'd have to start from Homer harbor, of course, which added an extra twelve miles to the journey, but that's where the water taxi vessel was.

Carrying in an armload of spruce to feed the carbon monoxide machine that December 4 morning, I allowed myself one last brief debate on the wisdom of my resolution: Hmmm.

"Cross the bay now," I asked myself, "when the annual cavalcade of fishing deaths is already well under way?" Hmmm.

An excursion like this one to my magical pond was my first real opportunity to acquire the affected Relaxed Tone, and a legitimate Step One event. (I saw sleeping away from home in the wintertime as a Step One issue because in such a situation one has to be able to master the concept of heat—to get a fire going wherever one is.) Never mind that death comes quickly in Alaskan waters: in ninety seconds for the thick-skinned. The key is to not fall in. It's barely four miles straight across from my cabin, but you don't want to be faced with swimming any part of it at all. Not even in the summer, when the bay's temperatures can soar to 45 degrees. Assuming you know the nasty quirks and currents and the water's calm, you'll make about fifty strokes before hypothermia kicks in. Hmmm.

Kachemak Bay embraces and dominates the Homer area landscape the way the Chesapeake Bay does Baltimore. All life around here eventually comes back to this body of water, which was a hop, skip, and jump from my door. Its surface, deceptively flat from a distance and ranging in hue from mint green to the deepest cerulean blue, lures like a siren's call.

✻ ✻ ✻ ✻ ✻

In retrospect, it might have been a good thing that I didn't know before I made the Cheechako-headed plans for this trip that another Homerite was about to meet his end in the bay. I didn't know because I was myself across the bay when it happened. I found out only after the event that a Russian fisherman drowned (or froze) when his boat flipped on him, at a spot closer even to the Homer harbor than I was at the time. It's not a rare event—there's a monument to the fallen fishermen of Alaskan waters on the Homer Spit—the jutting finger of land that houses the harbor.

True, there were two stories of the demise of the unfortunate fisherman. As told by Mako, the water taxi driver—who probably never knew he was the most important person in my life for a time in December—the fisherman's death was evidence of the barely navigable waters that I was reckless to traverse by choice in this foul season. The *Homer News* had a different take on things, however, saying the Coast Guard was investigating why someone's boat would bounce on top of him on "unusually calm waters." This seemed to me a euphemism for speculation about how much the fisherman had been drinking on his last day.

Re-Re-Confirming the Water Taxi

Whichever version one likes—and together they probably tell a fairly complete story of the dangers that face the would-be Alaskan Step One pursuer—the death might've been cause for strong reconsideration on my part if it had occurred a week earlier. Maybe. But in the end it probably wouldn't have deterred me. The way I was seeing it, I was taking important baby steps toward Mountain Manhood. While visiting a place that was already in my heart forever.

So in less than six and a third hours of official daylight on December 4, the plan was set in stone: across the bay for one night it was. There is only one way to cross Kachemak Bay in December if you don't own a boat. His name is Mako, the water-taxi driver, and he is an excellent boatman and a fine human being. The only thing about Mako is that he operates according to Homer O'clock. I knew this when I called him around noon on December 4 for a December 13 booking. That characteristic aside, I love hanging out with Mako (pronounced MAH-koe): he's witty, full of ideas, quick to laugh. He's also an incredibly knowledgeable movie buff and, most important, safe in the operation of his motor vessels. So Mako has a chronological inclination toward Homer O'clock. Big deal. Everything in Homer operates on the erratic groove of Homer O'clock. There's nothing anyone can do about it. Not even a conveyor of people and goods. Not even one who is dependent on tides and weather. Mako is simply one of those typically Homer-quirky people, living in one of the few English-speaking places in which nonmillionaires are allowed to be quirky and profitable. There is, in fact, a culture of quirkiness here.

Take JM. Most folks who knew about my level of Cheechakoness as of my first Alaskan December would have considered it something of a quirk that the minute she heard about this planned pond excursion, she was in.

JM is the toughest, most fearless outdoorsperson I have ever met. During our sledding date on the 4th, I raved in an amateur Relaxed

Tone about the prospect of icy waters and mountains of snow, all in pursuit of this one tiny frozen dreamscape pond in the wilderness. And her response was, "Hey, great. I just had my skates sharpened."

What would I do without these quirky people? As for my conveyance to the pond was concerned, if I couldn't predict exactly when we would make it over to my heavenly destination, I knew Mako would take us. This guy was down for anything; an optimist, a congenital supporter of dreams. I patiently allowed the seven-day waiting period for him to return my call.

"Yeah, dude, this is Mako," a hip, drawly voice twanged into the receiver on Friday, December 11, as I was sword-fighting an out-of-control fire. "Are you fucking crazy?"

"Crazy? What do you mean?"

"It's cold over there."

"And snowy," I tried to admit in a sort of Relaxed Tone. Learning from my Roger experience, I had timed it perfectly. Mako's Homer O'clock return call had come two days before what I envisioned would be Pond Ice-Skating Trip Day. But it also came after about five days of constant snowfall which trapped V-8 tow trucks in mid-ditch-pull.

"At least as snowy. Do you have snowshoes?"

"We have hip waders."

"We?"

"We."

"Party of Two?"

"Party of Two. Emphasis on party."

This seemed to compute with his winter accounting ledger. Not exactly the busy season for a water-taxi operator in Alaska. I was Free-Ranging, of course, acting as though whatever the bay and the winter had to throw at me would be within my "Comfort Zone."

I didn't really know what the bay and the winter would throw, which might have been for the best. A disorienting blizzard? A tender thaw? Somersaults on the bay at thirty knots? Ah, the blissful ignorance of Cheechakohood. As Laura knew, I wasn't prepared for anything more substantial than wood chopping. Mako probably recognized this. It takes a Free-Ranger to know one.

"OK. But Sunday?" Mako fired back at me. "I don't know, dude. That's the day after tomorrow. I'm supposed to be at (longtime homesteader) Yule (Kilcher)'s funeral. And right now I'm snowed in."

"OW! It has to be Sunday, for our schedules," I explained, lightheaded with smoke inhalation. The molten fire poker was starting to sear my hand, until the visiting JM took it from me. "We want to go at 8:00 A.M. The funeral is at one. You can get us there and be back in time. Man that mother is hot." This was the only way to deal with Homer O'clock: informing how it's going to be.

"Eight in the morning? Are you fucking crazy?"

I could detect that Mako seemed to have some objection. "What do you mean?" I inquired, with the pre-emphysemic strain of someone who lives with insufficiently ventilated wood heat.

"It'll be dark, dude."

"Yes, but it'll be sunrise by the time we get there, and we want to maximize daylight. We only have one day and a night. I've thought this through."

"Do you have a tent?"

"It's a little bit ripped. But yes."

"OK, listen. Call me Saturday night and we'll see what they're saying about the weather."

The confirmation call. I welcomed this development. It was just like booking travel with any indigenous person in any developing country. If you don't re-re-confirm, it's as if you never booked at all. But if you do, it lurches reality one level closer, like an electron level jump. It's the closest we ever come to prescribing our own future.

I hung up the phone immensely satisfied, feeling I had maneuvered Homer O'clock into an understanding of how I wanted things to unfold. Sunday was our day. JM had allotted herself a last day off before a block of work days at the flower shop. I had arranged my complex schedule of column writing and woodcutting.

I stepped out on the deck to dunk my pulsing hand in the snow and heard the phone ring. It was Roger calling, almost as soon as I hung up with Mako (suspiciously as soon, I now sometimes think). Cowed only slightly by Mako's reluctance to maneuver the bay, I took the opportunity to ask Roger, my principal Mountain Man advisor, what he thought of the wisdom of such a expedition, given current conditions.

"Go for it," he advised without a pause. The phone line scratched like a dyspeptic cat from some weather interference. Then Roger continued. "Say, have you ever heard the Traffic album *John Barleycorn Must Die?* Great stuff. You've got to come over and tape it from me."

The thing is, Roger would advocate leaping out of an airplane without a parachute in hopes of landing on a soft haystack, provided there was egg salad and Redknot waiting below. He might not have been the ideal consultant on this one.

Laura's take in the General Store was a little different. When I had made up my mind about the trip a week earlier, she had said, "Nice knowing ya."

* * * * *

I took Laura's farewell advice to mean that this trip required planning. My previous visits to the pond had come under 65 degree summer skies. I recognized that August's conditions in Southcentral Alaska bear about as much resemblance to December's as Tahiti's do. This was not going to be like a visit to the local hockey rink.

The planning began immediately on Saturday morning, the 12th. I gathered my hatchet. Extra socks. A Ziplock baggie full of dry twigs.

Re-Re-Confirming the Water Taxi

My preparations soon took over the whole cabin the way trip preparations do—in a jumble of lists and pre-pack piles. Ten hours after I got off the phone with Mako, I dug myself out of the cabin and found myself in Ulmer's Hardware in town. There I bought two toy fluorescent orange shovels (at $3.99 these were half the weight of the highly technical and equally plastic $64 ones sold at the trendy outdoor gear store in Anchorage).

"Will these things hold up to serious windchill?" I asked the former Army supply sergeant who runs the gun department at Ulmer's. The shovels were next to some semiautomatic Democrat-killers.

"Those are for toddlers," he answered, matter-of-factly. (Did Ulmer's talk to the saw store? Would they know the Chainsaw Story here?)

"Same weather for them," I pointed out.

"True enough," he agreed, and in his eyes there was muttering about liberals.

The plan was straightforward in the extreme: JM and I would remove snow cover from our glacial rink with these rain forest–handled, slave labor-constructed shovels. Then we would shred the pond ice with the steel of our skate blades. Then I would garner a Relaxed Tone by sleeping outside in the winter in Alaska. Then we would be picked up and returned first thing the next morning, in time for a work day.

But there were complications. First and most serious, I didn't know what to do about Sunny. If JM was instantly in on the pond trip, so was Sunny, in her own mind. I understood that I was a man blessed with two companions. A fellow can't ask for much more than that in life. It's just that the snow was a little deep for Sunny, not to mention for me. It was well above her head. When I was more familiar with backcountry Alaskan winter conditions, I'd bring her along without a second thought.

What finally made up my mind was watching my dog burrow

through the system of subterranean tunnels that the outdoor world had become for her after the recent storms. Her pace was literally a crawl as she dug her way across the woods like a mole. I was worried that she wouldn't be able to escape from some sleepy bear-with-the-munchies she awoke during her explorations across the bay.

Ugh. Breaking it to her wasn't easy. Sunny always knows when something fun is afoot. Something in my body language or some chemical I exude tips her off. And she loved the pond, too. She accepted the verdict under protest, by shooting me a heart-melting look that for me ended once and for all any debate about canine versus primate intelligence.

"It'll be an experiment," I explained as we wrestled in the snow. "If it doesn't seem too harsh, I'll bring you next time, I promise. It's for your own good."

That reluctantly decided, there was a further Homer O'clock road-block. Saturday night, Mako was not optimistic when I "confirmed" as scheduled. I wasn't surprised. Saturday had been the first day I'd ever paid attention to the marine weather forecast on KBBI. After moaning to JM for months about how long, boring, and needlessly detailed it was, I surprised her Saturday afternoon after the run to Ulmer's by complaining that the forecast should be read more often. For us seafarers.

I see now that this was evidence that I was no longer operating on any kind of rational basis. These kinds of plans get on autopilot in my head. If you stopped me midstream on, say, Saturday evening, I would have been as surprised as you were that I was seriously considering making a journey into the Alaska wilderness in December.

But I kept listening to the radio, hungry for weather information. Despite my new-found support, the marine forecast really wasn't necessary. Over the course of many jargon-laden, frightening paragraphs, the forecast that day was just saying the same thing it always did. In essence, "It's the subarctic. Storms come. Water's cold. Boat at your

Re-Re-Confirming the Water Taxi

own risk." I could tell that by looking at the snow barreling earthward outside my bay window. And Mako was not unaware of conditions either.

But gale warnings and twenty-foot seas (diminishing to six feet by morning) or not, Mako disclosed during my unsuccessful confirmation call that he had to go to his office hut on the Homer Spit in the morning (Sunday) anyway, to start his boats, for the same cold weather reasons people were starting their buried cars every couple of hours. We were welcome to meet him there above the A float on the Homer dock to inspect current weather conditions on the spot.

That sounded fair enough. There was still a chance of getting to the pond on Sunday. Saturday night JM and I finished packing on the floor of my cabin in a triage session beside an eyelash-singing fire. I was glowing with the sense of pride one assumes when sharing a place one loves—I spoke as though I had personally designed the pond on which we were to skate.

By contrast JM, a survivor, was all about business. She indicated right off that my hockey gloves and stick would have to be jettisoned. In a misguided attempt to distract her, I told her that Mako had two boats, one a tiny open Whaler, essentially a floating bathtub, and the other a bigger, twenty-seven-foot former fishing boat with a covered top enclosing the small cabin. It was a mistake to mention this. JM decided to fixate for the evening on which of the two he would use to churn us through frigid air and icy frothing surf. Her concern was not unreasonable. Sometimes Sunny and I would go to a remote beach and watch this froth. The marine weather forecast calls it "freezing spray"— that is the technical meteorological term.

Our first trip to the Homer Spit was a waste. Mako flat out refused to take us Sunday morning, the 13th. Too much snow and wind and freezing spray, he explained in a flurry of "fucking crazies" and "dudes." I can't say I totally disagreed with him. It looked horrible.

The marine weather forecast was busting out the usual "boat at your own risk" mantra as I stamped my boots on the kitchen mat when we returned from the harbor. It occurred to me at that moment that there are more small craft advisories than small craft on Kachemak Bay and nearby Cook Inlet, and the outlook is always for some kind of immorally high seas. I carried in some wood and settled back into the cabin, thinking my pond dream trip was stymied. But I almost had given in to the erratically ticking hands of Homer O'clock too soon.

"Be at my office at 10:00 A.M.," Mako told me resignedly Sunday night when I half-heartedly re-re-confirmed. We had worn him down. "That's when the tides are right anyway." He knew what capsizing meant. It meant a long and embarrassing Coast Guard search followed by "better them than me" thoughts among the mourners at the funerals.

In honor of our perseverance, JM decided to play hooky from work for one more day. She would start her shift Tuesday afternoon.

* * * * *

On the dozen-mile drive to the harbor and A float Monday morning, JM and I watched the bay and discussed whether the wind was severe. My take was that the water looked pretty calm: ripply but minimal whitecaps. Hers was that the harbor area was irrelevant, and we were supposed to watch the horizon for signs of wavering in the air currents or something. What the whole conversation neglected was that neither JM, nor myself, nor the hitchhiker we'd picked up and dropped near town, knew what the heck we were talking about. The discussion was making us nervous and bickery. I turned up the radio to distract us just in time to hear another unnerving marine weather forecast. I quickly switched off the radio, thinking that from here, at least, the day could only get better.

But there was another slight complication as soon as we parked on the spit above the Homer dock. JM was getting something out of her pack—lip balm I believe—so she only caught it out of her peripheral vision. But she later called it one of the most spectacular wipeouts she had ever witnessed.

What Mako saw, sitting in the one waterside shack among the boarded-up tourist shops and custom fish processors from which smoke was emerging, was so simple and abrupt that his eyes could hardly accept it: a vaguely familiar Cheechako approaching him determinedly, and then suddenly disappearing.

Running to the door and opening it, not ten feet from his front doorstep, he realized that the car's owner had fallen into a hole. A big but previously hidden crevasse in the snow. A black knit hat, of the Subcomandante Marcos variety and slightly off-kilter, slowly emerged, followed by the rest of the Cheechako, now bearing a distinct frosty aura literally from head to toe. The Cheechako shook snow out from his back, grimaced in obvious pain in what appeared to be his shoulder, and greeted him with a hearty, "Good morning."

Even at this early stage in my first winter, I had noticed (and once, late for deadline, in fact had written a column about) the odd, stooped posture assumed by many Alaskans during the frozen months. I called it The Walk. The reasons for The Walk were repeatedly suggested while I was parallel to the ground and eighteen inches above it, a surprisingly common position for me in 1998, given the Earth's gravitational force. When I fell into the hole outside Mako's shack this morning with JM, I had become so comfortable with falling that I was able to be analytical about it. "What's really surprising," I remember reflecting as gravity did its work, "is that Alaska liability insurance isn't higher."

How is it, I wondered as I braced for the painful crash, that every Alaskan doesn't fall at least once a winter in some horribly disfiguring and potentially actionable slip? I was starting to realize it's all about this subtle C-shape Alaskans assume when making their way across an ice-caked and frictionless parking lot or walkway. You have to know what to look for to recognize the posture—hands ever-so-slightly jutted out for balance, and legs widened for lowered center of gravity. I had not mastered The Walk by December 14, 1998.

I've had a lifetime to get used to my general balance problems, but each new incident continues to force a rough adjustment. I take it case by case, give thanks each time I find myself not paralyzed, and have learned to live with the embarrassment by arguing that not all animals have the opportunity to walk upright even some of the time.

Mako politely pretended that my fall hadn't shaken him. Without comment he led us down the A float to his slightly bigger boat, still small enough to cause me to look around for survival suits. I didn't see any. They must have been in a drawer somewhere. All vessels are equipped with the suits, which allow you to . . . well, survive for a few hours while the Coast Guard scours the seas for your sunken conveyance. But for some reason no one seems to anticipate launching into arctic waters, so few mariners ever prophylactically wear survival suits as though they were bathing suits. And those who don them before tragedy strikes seem disproportionately cursed with things like broken zippers.

Ill-maintained survival suits had been the cause of several deaths in Alaska already that year, I recalled, rubbing the shoulder still aching from the slip. They were becoming an issue in public safety announcements on the radio. I climbed aboard and stood in the center of Mako's boat, shivering. I tried to imagine a worse feeling than fumbling hopelessly with the defective zipper of your survival suit while your deckhand tumbles over the stern to float in safety. Broken zippers are frustrating enough even when fighting them isn't your last living activity. "Boat at your own risk" indeed. Such was my mental state as Mako fired up his engines.

I looked over at the skipper working the helm and his serenity calmed me. You had to hand it to Mako in the style category: the tiny

Re-Re-Confirming the Water Taxi

cabin of this larger boat had work gloves clothespinned explicitly by the middle finger to a line near the helm. Beside his charts and maps there lay a copy of *The Nation* weighted down from the upsetting pressures of the maritime wind with a rock and a package of herbal tea. Like most people in Homer, Mako is some indistinguishable place between twenty-five and fifty-five years old.

Somewhat reassured by the orderly surroundings, I then made the mistake of glancing over the side of the boat as Mako flipped final switches and untied final lines, and thought to myself, "ninety seconds." My life expectancy in these waters. Never mind that Sunny will jump into Kachemak Bay in any season and swim as if it were a wading pool.

Poor Sunny. I missed her so much I had almost turned around during the drive to the harbor. You want to hang out with your best friend, not show her the pictures later. Since moving to Alaska, this was the first time that I had gone anywhere fun without Sunny accompanying me. It would happen again—this is reality in Alaska—but the first time is the hardest. She'd been outside since I woke up this Monday morning, so it wasn't like she'd be uncomfortable. On the contrary, the cabin floor was covered with a veritable golden retriever buffet. In a last minute fit of remorse, I'd left her with enough food, water, and peanut butter biscuits for a week. Not bad for one day's eatin', I supposed. But a poor substitute for joy.

These thoughts were interrupted when I noticed we were in motion. Once out of the harbor and heading east, in the cabin of the former fishing vessel JM and I both immediately assumed the casual pose of people trying not to appear seasick. We were moving along roughly the same route I take to my cabin out of Homer, only a few thousand yards south, which placed us in the bay instead of on East End Road. The boat's hull was taking monumental Eddie the Eagle ski jumps on the crest of nine-foot waves and then smashing with a sickening thunk back on the cement surface of the clay-gray water.

"Do you think Tom Cruise was miscast in *Born on the Fourth of July?*" Mako asked cheerfully from the helm.

"Mfff," I said, in what I suppose could have sounded like a Relaxed Tone, "Slightly, but Stone was thinking box office."

Thirty seconds had passed since I dropped a glove, but I could not take my eye off the horizon to pick it up. I put my arm around JM in an attempt to pretend that this was a routine ride, but she was too busy pretending to be engrossed by a spot on the water to respond with more than a forced smile. Mako reached around through a crack in the hatchway to chip ice off the windshield and in so doing permitted a cascade of sea water to smack me in the face. Bracing. I shook it off like Captain Ahab. I like this, I told myself.

"I don't know, dude," Mako said in a less chipper tone twenty minutes later as the boat fishtailed unnervingly and spun us toward Anchorage. "I don't like the look of this wind. I don't think I can get you ashore at your pond trail without damaging the boat."

I noticed a hopeful glimmer in JM's eyes. She clutched a bundle of sweater at my hip.

"I wouldn't want you to do anything to damage your boat," I managed to say. "But what's so tough about the wind now as opposed to ten minutes ago?" Despite my tenuous hold on my breakfast, I was still strongly dedicated to both my Step One progress and my pond.

"I just don't know if I could get close enough to drop you off." Mako was yelling now, because of the engine struggling with the water. "It's pretty shallow over there at the mouth of that creek where you hop off, and if the wind blows me ashore I could get stuck on the gravel and mess up the hull."

This sounded hazily familiar. "But you never get me right to the shore," I lobbied, pointing at my waders, which I had bought just for this purpose. "Could you get as far as you can and I'll jump out, and carry the gear to dry land over my head?" In my mind, I was picturing Normandy.

Re-Re-Confirming the Water Taxi

Mako was evidently impressed with my Free Ranging. "We'll take a look," he said.

Twenty nauseating seconds later Mako made a pronouncement. "We're going to Halibut Cove, dude." For punctuation, the boat slammed down into the trough of a wave, precipitating both a mild neck whipping and another bracing wash of seawater across my head. I was at the perfect angle for the bath, unable to move if I wanted to keep my bagel in my belly. Everyone else was dry. JM was in a trance, eyes closed.

I knew about Halibut Cove. It was a popular summer put-in spot with a quiet, protected lagoon several miles from the pond trail. It might have been Iowa. We were talking about two different trips.

As he veered south I shook off the nasty suspicion that Mako planned to abort the mission as soon as he saw me fall in the hole outside his office. "If this guy can't walk from the parking lot, it wouldn't do to unleash him on what is already the harshest winter in a quarter century," I imagined was his thought process. "The girl would probably make it."

It felt suspicious that Mako could judge the wind at the pond's dropoff creek from five miles away. I also noticed that he had made the unilateral decision at the precise moment he needed to turn south for Halibut Cove.

The water almost immediately became bathtub calm. I felt my nausea dissipate. Maybe this was the right decision. As we worked our way into the Halibut Cove lagoon, Mako became a political action committee for how "just as good" this place was.

"Dude, it's beautiful here. This is one of the most popular places I drop people in the summer. But it'll be like Swiss Family Robinson now. There'll be no one in the West Cabin. There's no one within miles and miles of here. I've never even been here at this time of year."

I was thinking about my jade pond, my glacial skating mission. "I

called the State Park people," I told him. "They said all the public cabins are closed."

"Closed or locked?" Mako asked.

"Locked, I assumed." I had decided to be resentful. "Plus don't they
cost like $50 per day even when they are open?"

* * * * *

"Dude, you were planning to tent camp anyway, right?" Mako was
moving at a pretty sharp clip through the Eden-like lagoon. About a
thousand terrified kittiwakes planed into the glare of the chalk-white
mountains encircling us like an amphitheater. "There's a lake only a
mile or two into the woods here, too, and it'll be protected by trees. You
won't have too much snow to clear off before you skate." He eyed the
toy shovels strapped to my pack, the kind designed to make a three-
year-old think he's "helping."

I was listening to some degree of Free-Range Bullshitting here, and
I accepted that. When you hear Free Ranging nearly every day, you not
only become inured to it after throwing traditional truth barometers
like cleanliness of speaker and exactitude of detail out the window, you
feel you can sift through it in real time, gleaning from a conversation
what information feels of value.

In this case, though, not having visited the spot Mako was describing,
I had no way to gauge what he was saying. I did, however, remember how
hard he had also sold the trail that led to the glacial pond before I had first
gone there. He had been right on the money that time; maybe he would
be again. Although I recalled that when first discussing the pond trail back
in June, we had every option open to us, and had considered them all in
front of a map in his office—both of us in shorts.

Mako was still lobbying from the helm as we penetrated deeper
into the heart of the lagoon, which made me think he wasn't so sure
himself. "There's a trail and everything," he said.

Re-Re-Confirming the Water Taxi

"That's also part of the problem," I explained, and here I felt I was on stronger ground. "There's, what, three feet of snow on the ground, at least, and I've never been here. I know the trail to my pond. I could find it with my eyes closed, or worst case I could follow the creek to the old hunter's cabin and we could shelter there. I could break into it with my hatchet if need be. Here I don't even know if I could find the trail."

We let that one sit for a while.

"It'll be fun, a test," a voice said from inside many sweaters. It was JM, still green, but emerging.

"Having a good time?" I asked.

"It's beautiful here."

"How're you feeling?"

"Better. As long as I don't think, move, or breathe."

"Look," Mako said from the helm. "Starboard side. Three o'clock."

A family of first one, then two, then five or six porpoises was greeting us with syncopated dives. An eagle flapped with furious whumps above a snow-weighted spruce and briefly eclipsed the faded whiskey sun. Suddenly we were in what for all of us was our favorite place: wilderness. Ahhhh.

After another ten minutes of increasingly good attitude on everybody's part, the boat nudged into the icy south edge of the lagoon, and JM and I hopped out. We ran up and down a frozen flight of stairs to the lagoon-edge cabin (which was unlocked), unloading and chatting with a sun-bathing Mako whenever we came down. I foolishly had my waders peeled down to my ankles during this process, and the snow I thus dragged into them was crystallizing my feet. The socks had already been soaked by the personalized splashes the bay had reserved for me during the ride across. It couldn't have been warmer than 10 degrees.

"No, Mr. Bond, I expect you to die," Mako said, by way of a quiz on my fourth trip down.

"*Goldfinger*," I answered, picking up my fanny pack and nearly falling into the lagoon. "Much has changed on the force since you went crazy."

"*Pink Panther Strikes Again.*" He was good. Clouseau's update to Former Chief Inspector Dreyfus at the sanitarium seemed particularly relevant to me just then.

Five more minutes passed, and following parting words with our water-taxi driver we got all of our gear up the stairs. As I dug in my pack for a change of socks on the cabin's lagoon-facing deck, JM elbowed me and we watched Mako's boat diminish to a silent dot. Then we looked at the sky and then at each other, with glances that said, "Dang. This is a big state. And cold." A snowflake landed ceremoniously on my nose. The sky was clouding over.

＊ ＊ ＊ ＊ ＊

By the time we slung our laced-together skates on our shoulders, it was after 1:00 P.M. Monday, December 14. There were three hours of direct light left. And the days were only getting shorter. We shrugged and started wandering around the lagoon fairly aimlessly, looking for the trail. Then we tried fairly organized expanding circles. By 3:15 we hadn't found the trailhead.

One thing about massive snowfalls: everything in the terrain looks like snow. The state park map in the cabin was no help in finding the lake: it was a vague indicator of general direction, not useful for thirty-six inches of virgin snow. Streams weren't marked. Curves weren't really marked. It was designed for summer, when you could see the trail.

Movement wasn't easy: our feet sank into each step as though the world were filled with hidden holes that came up to our thighs. And extracting ourselves from each stride was more difficult than going in had been. It made every step like climbing. When we wanted some pace, the motion was more like fire walking.

The atmosphere as we wandered, though brisk to say the least, and now snowing steadily, was delightfully clean. Each gulp of air felt as though it had healthy side effects as it frosted my trachea. But my spirit wasn't at peace after two hours in the backcountry. The more I thought about it, the more I was haunted by elements of our departing conversation with Mako. After JM and I had leaped onto shore with our last load, he had said, uncleating his line, "See you later. I can usually get into this lagoon, usually. But they're saying 80 percent chance of snow tonight. I don't know about the wind."

Why two "usually"s?

"10:00 A.M., then," JM had said, having had plenty of her own experience with Homer O'clock. "I have work tomorrow afternoon."

"Wait for me a little bit longer than that," Mako then needlessly reminded us, already pulling away and growing smaller. "The tide's getting later." And then he was gone.

As the light faded now one hundred minutes later, I had a twinge of fear about what would happen if Mako couldn't get to us. JM and I would be alone and stranded somewhere in the 586,412 square miles of basically wilderness that is rural Alaska. And this wasn't even the patch of the wilderness I wanted to be in.

* * * * *

Like a curmudgeonly member of the House of Lords, I was still mumbling about the fact that I couldn't skate on the pond I wanted, and there was almost no daylight in which to find anything at all to skate on, when we found a bend in the lagoon, JM put her mittened hand on my shoulder, and our world became what was happening now. We had company.

For perhaps the next forty minutes all we did was communicate with the porpoises. They swam amazingly close to shore, so close we could see their black bodies under the surface ten feet away. Immersed like lawn gnomes in the snow, JM and I summoned them with joyful shouts and they were more than willing to have a summit meeting. This was a world so completely quiet, their snorkel-like exhalations sounded like they could start an avalanche. In fact, for a while, breathing—theirs and ours—was the only sound to puncture the lagoon. To my mind, this sensation is better than the best drug.

Then I tried to ask if it were true that they had come out of the water, figured something out, and returned. Given how cold I tended to get outdoors in the subarctic, I was amazed that they had chosen the waters here. For the same reason I had, probably: this was a remnant of Eden.

JM and I eventually realized that if we were going to get any ice skating in, we would have to move on. It was close to 4:00 P.M. What shadows managed to form were already long. I noticed the snow was shaded gray as I scooped up a handful to drink.

I took a deep breath. "OK. Should we try to find the lake?"

JM looked at me and smiled. We chatted with the porpoises a little longer. The day shifted another notch. Any official trail was not visible. We'd never been here before. Another five minutes passed. We were losing light.

＊ ＊ ＊ ＊ ＊

Ten minutes later JM and I finally dragged ourselves away from the lagoon's porpoises, after a brief debate about becoming aquatic. Somehow it wasn't overly disconcerting to me anymore that the skating lake could be in any direction, at any distance. Plopped into a dense spruce forest, I wasn't even exactly sure what direction I was facing. And I didn't care.

There is something intoxicating about the very geology of this part of Southcentral Alaska—it's a whole different tectonic plate from the Kenai Peninsula back across Kachemak Bay, which joins the road system and connects Homer to Anchorage. There are places in the world—I don't know how or why—made for happiness. The difference

Re-Re-Confirming the Water Taxi

between Homer and the other side of the bay is the difference between seeing and being. You get a wider vista in Homer but you feel more across the bay. When some folks head across the bay, they call it "the other side." They might as well call it "the other planet."

So we set off again, vaguely away from the lagoon. My first footfall sucked me so deep into a root system I lost my balance. JM found this quite funny. In the middle of this snowstorm that Monday afternoon, I was feeling like a little kid, playing in the snow. That I was toting two bright orange mini-shovels might have helped. Plus my boots were too tight and my nose was running. When I saw JM's white figure skates bonking into her snow-speckled sweater with every step, I had no doubt we'd find our destination. Never mind that we were probably several miles from it and we couldn't find the trail. I had let go of all desire. I was going with whatever the day brought.

Just as that thought was forming in my head, I halfheartedly suggested that an undulation arcing southish into the woods, which we had earlier rejected, now felt like a trail. JM had to concede this point when we dug up a tree that had clearly been sawed off to allow passage. We had found the trailhead. It was just after sunset. My stomach leaped with the exhilaration of an unexpectedly successful mission.

But we soon reached a dead end, and it was getting, in this part of the world near winter solstice, late. The universe was the color of cardboard. That's when teamwork kicked in. I was absolutely ready to give up, and my body language showed it, when at the last miraculous moment, JM pointed up through a cluster of devil's club and said softly, "Is that a sign?"

It was, in more ways than one. Plunging through an absurd incline of thigh-deep snow, we came to a bear-shredded sign post. One of those varnished carved jobs that told us we were on a trail. Energized anew, we beat ahead through a field of now waist-deep snow, got disoriented in a tangle of spruce almost immediately, lost the top of the hot chocolate thermos, and realized we really had to turn back because of darkness.

After we had dug around fruitlessly for the thermos top for a few minutes, JM and I looked at each other with the regret of children who hear their mother calling. She was at her prettiest: snow flecked her hat and flakes were melting on her flushed cheeks. I just wanted to hug her, right then and there. So I did.

We felt like we had just got here. We had taken a few steps up the trail, and it was already time to head back. It wasn't anyone's fault; we had just set off and arrived late. But even our Plan B wasn't coming to fruition: if we had wanted to stroll, we could've taken a walk around the forest in Fritz Creek. We had both wanted to skate. Near the end of this abbreviated trip to Halibut Cove, we wished we'd had more time.

"I almost hope Mako doesn't come," JM said, chuckling to show she was just joking. "I feel like we're close to the lake."

"He'll come," I said uncertainly.

"Of course he has to come," JM said, and chuckled a little too forcefully this time. "I have to work in the afternoon."

I already knew that. I wondered why she felt the need to mention it again.

In retrospect, what I find notable about this conversation is that we doubted something so basic to our survival as an on-time (or even an on-day) winter pick-up. I wasn't sure whether that was because of our deep respect for the Alaskan weather, or because of our deep respect for Homer O'clock. But we weren't worrying about that for long as we waded back toward the lagoon. We were too happy. The local tectonics were kicking in again. Squirrels told jokes. Snowflakes recited vertical verse. We couldn't stop laughing. It was like that *Star Trek* episode where the crew goes on shore leave and gets all strung out on that tryptamine-laden plant.

We got back to the cabin in the last light. By flashlight I chopped a

Re-Re-Confirming the Water Taxi

familiar amount of wood and JM gathered kindling: the cabin, amazingly, guilt-inducingly, had a stove. As I stacked a small pile of spruce outside the door, JM stalked and ambushed me, causing us both to roll down a long hill leading from the cabin to a frozen creek bed.

We hooted and tackled each other, and collapsed in deep snow every time we tried to stand up. I kneeled on the creek, hopped once or twice to test its solidity, and howled fiercely at the moon, which was above the snowflakes somewhere. The falling snow seemed to appear out of a different dimension at a height of one foot. It took a very long time to gather an evening's worth of wood.

With our tromping in and out, the cabin floor was soon so wet with melting snow that it was almost a pool. I strung some bear rope we had brought along as an indoor clothesline. JM cut a strip of it to use as a makeshift belt for her old-school Swiss Army wool jodhpur trousers, which were warmer, of course, than my Space Age fibers. We were already starting to lose weight.

Chapter 4
Surviving on Polysorbate 80

JM and I sipped hot chocolate on the lagoonside deck in the dark, confused by the battle between time and natural rhythm: her watch said one thing (6:20 P.M.), and we felt another (midnight). Almost invisible songbirds darted overhead singing a faint staccato fugue. It was difficult for any sound to penetrate this ethereal atmosphere. When I howled, it came right back to me, the sound waves damp and slightly mushy. Light, too, was enveloped by inky darkness a few inches from our flashlights. The wind chilled our noses.

Still outside, we ate a hearty dinner of processed instant pasta, beef jerky, and Cup-a-Soup, thus having quickly achieved our sodium requirement for 1999. At one point JM waited until I took a bite of jerky to say, "I made sure to get the kind that was made with beef hearts. Notice how it sticks together in perfect tubes."

That prompted me to check the ingredients. "What's Polysorbate 80?" I asked, grimacing as the gritty intestinal mush spread thickly across my tongue. "And what went wrong with Polysorbates 1 through 79?"

"You don't want to know," she said, and she was probably right. How many sorbates does the healthy adult need? Could the FDA be trusted for an honest answer? It was not my most indigenous moment. When I tested later and discovered that Sunny—a scavenging pack animal who eats lettuce—didn't recognize the jerky as food, I made a mental note to learn how to smoke my own meat. But I wasn't really anywhere close yet to Step Two: Food Gathering.

Reluctantly we returned from the deck with bellyaches and hunkered down for the evening. Eventually the refrigerated excuse for a cabin, new but recognizably porous, warmed up a bit with our wet wood burning. With cracks visible, it had been hastily built with *Exxon Valdez* oil spill criminal settlement money that removed much of this forest from the clear-cut docket.

And what a cabin. Each time we had gotten turned around on a false trail during the afternoon lake search and returned to look at the ambiguous map on the cabin wall (the mere existence of maps proved this a more "developed" wilderness than our intended pond destination, at least in summer), I marveled at how chilled I got by going *inside*. Only in the cabin could I see my breath, which seemed contrary to the concept of "in." Maybe this was why the cabin hadn't been visited for more than three months, according to the guest registry. More frighteningly, it reminded me of something—oh, yes, my own cabin.

"Just like home," I commented to JM as we got ready for bed, and it sounded like some kind of hotel chain slogan in *The Twilight Zone*.

Still, I was ashamed of the stove. This trip was about skating, yes. But it was supposed to prove something about survival, about taking steps toward Mountain Manhood. I felt guilty about the whole idea of walls, and during dinner we discussed setting up the tent, on the basis of principles we couldn't name. Then, following one last snowball fight, we looked around us at the forest as it continued to gently snow us into a winter wonderland. There must've been hundreds of snowflakes out there. After dinner we stopped discussing the tent.

Instead, as the eight o'clock hour approached, we talked in hushed voices about snow days like this one in our childhoods. "All other time stops when they give you a snow day," JM said. "Nothing else matters but the snow."

"And if the power goes out, you get to light candles," I said. "It's like a campout right at home."

It was around 11:00 P.M. when we finally collapsed into a pile of sleeping bags that night. There was a loft in the cabin, and that's where we made camp, like eagles. Still high from the other side of the bay, a fair amount of tickling ensued. Eventually, our evening ended. We hadn't skated, but it had been a fun trip. A snow day. We could always come back when we had more time.

* * * * *

By noon it was pretty clear Mako wasn't going to show. But we made the mistake of waiting until that point to collect more wood and again didn't set off on the lake search until after 1:00 P.M. Following wilderness etiquette, we wanted to be sure we left enough fire fodder for the next visitors to get started (even if we were the next visitors), but we went far beyond that. Based on what we had learned the previous night about the breathable cabin walls and supersaturated floor, we knew anyone who stayed here during the winter would need a vast supply of fuel.

In the cabin I recall that we conveyed remarkable matter-of-factness—on the surface—about our unplanned second afternoon across the bay. Before it had really sunk in for me that we were looking at at least twenty-four extra hours in the December wilderness, JM had her still-damp jodhpurs pulled on and her skates slung over her shoulder. I followed her conceptual lead, which seemed to be, "We're here to skate. Let's find the darn lake."

The only problem with that theory is that we had even less daylight to work with than we had the previous day. We would have to almost jog the whole time—which conditions didn't allow—and even then we probably wouldn't find the lake unless the trail were suddenly marked with a yellow neon stripe. So we almost knew we weren't going to get there, but we didn't want to sit around, letting the realization that we were castaways grow on us. We were both committed to this logical idiocy. It was simply a case of, "What else are you going to do when stranded in the subarctic wilderness, waiting for your lift home?" Maybe if we didn't give ourselves time to think about the possibilities, we wouldn't. It was only when I climbed down from the loft scratching my head after a search for my hat that I had a moment to think, "Is this serious? How serious is this?"

$$* * * * *$$

After JM doled out the lunch sodium, we set off following the remnants of our earlier tracks, now more like circular squirrel marks than human prints. I had the odd feeling as I passed the frozen creek that I remembered howling at the moon, but didn't feel like howling anymore.

At the sawed-off tree we started in with bursts of old television and movie dialogue. We tried to see how many commercial slogans back we could remember for major consumer products. It was easier for me: JM hadn't even had a TV for much of her childhood. This banter wasn't a good sign. Yesterday we hadn't had time for conversation—we were too immersed in the other side of the bay. It seemed clear immediately in the silent wooded universe that the reality of the missed rendezvous weighed upon us. Upon me, at least. Joking around was a sort of reverse psychology: pretend everything was OK. It's amazing to me in retrospect how naturally and wordlessly we agreed to this. Or maybe JM just felt like joking around.

It became a game: try to make every sentence a reference to some sort of commercial jingle or a line from a movie we had watched together.

"When they said it was snowy over here, they said it all," JM commented, stepping over the tree. "Which reminds me. When You Say Bud, You've Said It All."

"Did you know that British Petroleum is the Number One Investor in Alaskans?" I asked, citing a protest-too-much advertising campaign.

JM needed to tie a bootlace when we passed the bear-shredded trail sign. This gave me a few seconds to notice that I felt a peculiar emotion, somewhere between fatalistic and concerned. We were both at this point undeniably in constant awareness of the prospect of having been abandoned in the wilderness. But if it weighed upon the recesses of my mind, it hadn't fully hit home in the frontal lobes. To me, it felt like an impossibly Cheechakoey way to die. What would the coroner say when our corpses were found in the spring? "Death By Homer O'clock?" Would gossipy speculation erupt surrounding why we were carting around two children's shovels? I thought that if we were going to die, we should make it look like we starved, rather than froze. Famine occurs in many indigenous societies, especially ones with consumer prices as high as Alaska's. When one is considering one's last impression on the obituary page, there is a sort of prestige to starving that freezing lacks.

It couldn't have been much later than 1:45 when we reached our farthest point of the previous day, the mashed-down snow where the Thermos top was last seen. We rested for a moment, and each gave the other a quick look that I took to say, "Now is your chance to call this off." JM adjusted her skates over her shoulder. I scoured ahead through the already darkening woods at a dubious but possible route to the lake.

The break over, JM and I crouched down and dug into the ground like forensic scientists. I put my ear down as though I might be one of those people who can hear a trail. Following a circuitous twenty-minute search, we actually did pick up the trail again, after thinking for a difficult quarter mile that we must be bushwhacking. Russian hats of snow fell off trees on our heads if we made too much noise as we trudged in loops, continually losing and refinding the route. We tried to time our noise so as to splash the other's head, which I took as a promising indication of state of mind. The other side of the bay wasn't going to let our spirits drop too far. But I was watching for any psychic indication of impending mental collapse in either one of us.

After another hour of tough snow work and many false trails, we came to the branch-off point, not more than a half mile from our cabin

Surviving on Polysorbate 80

as the raven flies, separating the path to a ranger station from the trail that led to our skating lake. We had trudged at least two miles on dead ends and phantom trails. We dropped down for a rest right at the crossroads. I felt that incongruous winter combination of sweat and chill as JM checked her watch.

"Well, that was a productive day," she said.

"The best part of getting lost," I sang, "is Folgers in your cup."

Already it was again time to head back for solar angular reasons. We were maybe halfway from our cabin to the lake, at best. I felt layers of disappointment overlapping each other; I couldn't tell which one was predominant at any moment: that we couldn't skate where we wanted, that we couldn't skate at all, or that we couldn't get back to our homes. As we lay munching raisins in the idyllic snowfall, drained from the uphill/downhill/uphill aerobics, JM was strategizing.

"The ranger station probably has radio equipment," she speculated casually. A snowflake balanced on her attractively pouty lower lip. "We could tell someone to see what's up with our ride."

I analyzed that statement for a long time before answering. All was still calm on the surface, but I felt she might be testing the psychic waters as well. We weren't doing TV commercials anymore. I wasn't sure that she had broken the ice in her choice of subject matter, but I don't think she realized that I was balancing precariously close to the edge of pretending this was still fun, still a skating trip. Were we advancing into a kind of emotional Code Yellow, one step short of emergency?

"What makes you say that?" I asked finally, keeping my tone jocular. "There's not supposed to be anybody here till spring. This forest's closed."

"You think they take the radio back with them to the Homer side for the winter and bring it back when they return?"

"Wouldn't you?"

"I guess," she admitted, and blew her nose. For a couple of minutes we continued to psychoanalyze the likely behavioral patterns of the Alaska state ranger for this district, whom JM knew.

* * * * *

A woodpecker tapped out a polyrhythmic rumba above us on a spruce. I offered it some raisins, then listened to its Morse code as though for instructions. JM wedged up to me and snuggled into my allegedly waterproof shoulder. I caught snowflakes on my tongue. This is always more of a satisfaction than it warrants, skill-wise.

"What do you reckon the temperature is?" JM asked.

"Five?" I guessed. "Seventeen?"

"Something like that. I feel warm, though."

"Me, too. Except my toes."

"Me too."

"Next time let's bring a compass and a good map," I suggested.

"And a thermometer," JM added. "And, um, garlic. And a gun."

"That really would alter the whole scenario, wouldn't it?" I philosophized. "Our whole positioning in the food web. But I'm for it."

"Moose roast," she pointed out suggestively. We hadn't brought very much food.

"Squirrel," I proposed.

"Porpoise. Just kidding. (Pause.) We wouldn't be able to swim out and retrieve the carcass, anyway. Too cold." One of our stomachs gurgled. In a perfectly silent world, one takes notice of such things.

I was lucky to be here with JM, I realized. Besides her levelheaded sturdiness, she was fun. I don't really even know how we came together so . . . exclusively. We started having meandering, all-night conversations in June about cheesecake recipes and telecommunications deregulation, and suddenly her spare toothbrush was in my bathroom. Lately she had started sharing her life story with me without feeling she had a patent on pain. I liked her philosophy about life in general. She seemed to be living it. Period.

It occurred to me at this odd moment, this surreal mixture of romantic pleasure and fear for our lives, that traditionally, my concerns right about now should be those of the trucker at the Down East Saloon: whether this was all still within my life-or-death Comfort Zone. The trucker had felt he might've survived about twelve more hours if that whiteout hadn't cleared. JM and I were looking at considerably more than twelve hours; twenty hours, at least, if Mako both remembered us and could get in with the tide the following day. Of course, in the cabin we had heat. But what surprised me is that I found I wasn't worrying about the supposedly core traditional things when I was lost in the Alaskan wilderness. Things like frostbite. Carrion fowl. Neptune-like windchill. It's only afterward that the adventure literature jibes with what I was actually experiencing. When life gets real, I was finding, the need to Free Range diminishes.

Instead, as we rested and ate raisins, I worried about things like, "Is my girlfriend hogging the raisins?" and even "Boy, some hot chocolate would sure taste good right now." I think this is why comparisons to legend annoy many contemporary Alaskans. Everyone's just trying to live—to make it through that day. If conditions turn harsh, what did you expect? This ain't California. This is Alaska.

While JM sat up and adjusted her rope belt, I thought about the physiology of our bodies just wanting to concentrate on being satisfied now. I can't describe how much I appreciated this clever adaptation, for the few minutes it lasted. It allowed my mind to steer away from panic at the long-term situation. "One moment at a time," seems to be the biological message.

For a little while. Slowly, however, I couldn't help thinking ahead, as we digested our snack. Maybe with the body temporarily satisfied, my mind had space to wander. I did some math. Okay, Mako was only four and a half hours late and had only missed one pickup at this point. Only one. Just one. But uncertainty is one of the key ingredients in fear. If one day, why not two? If two, why not a whole winter? He was supposed to have been here at 10:00 that morning. What would we feel if noon came around again the next day, and we were still staring at the now-familiar porpoises? Perhaps by way of psychological preparation, I was almost living that third day sinking feeling, at 2:30 P.M. on the second day.

An uninvited thought leaped into my head. Maybe Mako was testing me. Maybe this was some kind of Cheechako rite of passage. Had Roger been in touch with Mako, letting him know how much I had to learn about survival? I wasn't sure they even knew each other. But what if they did? Like Cato being instructed to attack Inspector Clouseau in order to keep him constantly on his toes, maybe some of my friends, knowing of my expressed quest to join them in Mountain Manhood, had prepared some real-world obstacle courses for me. I checked my pack to see if any notes or treasure maps had been slipped in there. There were none. I sighed. When planning this trip, I had envisioned a Step One introduction, not some kind of harrowing Sisyphean effort.

JM at this moment leaned over and whispered, "It has been really nice knowing you." Then she bounded to her feet playfully and, faking a move into the woods, jumped on me. "Don't worry about avalanches!" she screamed, to see if she could get more snow to fall on my head from the surrounding trees. Then she sprang up and started sprinting farther up the trail.

"Let's skate," she called.

"In the dark?"

"Whatever it takes," she said, before spinning around with a smile in her eyes. She reached me and sweetly added, "Just kidding."

Her jocularity surprised me. It was difficult to tell what JM was thinking in survival situations versus, say, on an afternoon stroll. She attacked everything with the same paced, sensible deadpan and big, watchful coal-black pupils, and only later on (usually after returning) revealed what she found notable or absurd. When traveling with me it almost always had to do with my behavior or marginally functional cerebellum. It was pretty rare that she would burst forth with outright silliness. I didn't know what to make of it.

And so on that note we started the sloshy hike back to the cabin for the second time. It turned out to be trickier than the previous day's return, because we weren't sure which of our many widely experimental turns represented the correct route cabinward, and because we were so much farther away. Plus, we were getting exhausted and borderline hypothermic. My legs felt like lead—as heavy as they had felt light the previous afternoon—and I'm convinced I was in general starting to exude something other than my outward happy-go-luckiness.

By 3:30 P.M., when we followed our own false trail almost back to the ranger station crossroads, JM's inner smile seemed wiped off her face, too. I think. My eyes were fusing shut with every blink, which was affecting my vision, and my right nostril had frozen closed. An hour before we finally returned to the bear-shredded sign, we had reached what I see now was a middle ground between levelheadedness and panic.

I started to envision a winter in Halibut Cove. Not enjoying the images that were coming to mind, I called out every television catch phrase I could remember. JM joined me. Underneath all the joking around now lurked questions so clear I could almost hear them. Was the pressure getting to us? Where was Mako? Was he hibernating? Drowned on the way back to Homer? Unable to tear himself away from some endless Warhol film? Or had it simply been weather that delayed him?

Could he simply have forgotten about us? For a while it seemed the next logical dimension of Homer O'clock: complete ignoring of all responsibility and commitment. Mako had kids, a house. Perhaps these superseded the lives of business relationships. But as overpowering a dynamic as Homer O'clock was, wasn't it, like everything, relative? Couldn't sufferers discern differences in time-sensitiveness between, say, stove installation appointments and more survival-dependent activities like say, frigid winter snowstorm pickups in the backcountry?

"Okay, Okay. Keep it together," I thought, shivering in the serious way righteous Victorian period films with Winona Ryder portray people with the ague. "Don't get carried away. The boat is only seven hours overdue." Mako was essentially the only one who knew we were out here. I may have informed my column editor, who was unlikely to worry unless I missed a couple of deadlines. But who would she call, anyway? 911 in the 907 area code? Did that work?

Tromping back through the forest at 4:40 P.M., snow piling into my waders as I took an ill-advised step on a dubious foothold, we lapsed into an overwhelming silence. Finally I asked, "Do people send Bush Lines saying things like, 'If anyone's seen Doug call the Forest Service'?"

"Yes, they do all the time," JM answered, seeing my point so quickly that the thought had to have been on her mind. Then she added a little plaintively, "But who would do that for us?"

She wouldn't be missed at work because she had skipped most of the previous week with the flu. Sue, her boss at the flower shop, had told her to come back when ready, and "ready" was going to be after our excursion. I looked behind me and noticed that JM had devised a method of stepping on protruding clumps of devil's club to get better footing. I toyed with the idea of arguing with her for not enlightening me about the system, but decided to let it drop.

The snow picked up as dusk descended and we seemed to be getting close to the cabin; smaller, colder flakes polka-dotted us now. As we arced around a strip of pseudo-trail leading to a ravine on which I had misdirected us once already, I wanted to whine about the pain in my overworked legs. But instead I told myself to "have a good attitude." I thought I had said it quietly.

Surviving on Polysorbate 80

"What?" JM, a pretty snowwoman in her nerdy military trousers, asked behind me.

"Much has changed on the force since I went crazy," I explained, dredging up the Clouseau line from the pre-disappearance exchange with Mako. I was referring to myself, but JM, probably feeling the same inner uncertainty I was, wasn't smiling. In fact, her face registered an eerily absolute absence of expression.

"Have a Coke and a smile," she observed dryly.

* * * * *

We made it back to the cabin that second evening after the world had turned to India ink. It was 6:15 P.M. We were lucky to have been so close to home base when the long twilight mocha suddenly transformed into absolute, pre-Creation darkness. I was peeling off my layers absentmindedly when I looked at JM, and was worried by what I saw. In front of the stove, she was watching with an expression of fascination as the sweat-induced steam rose off her thermaled thighs. As if transfixed, she said without looking up, "Our entire lives are dependent on the short-term memory of this one man. We should've told more people we were going. They would've understood."

There was nothing in her tone that was even pretending to be lighthearted. Up until this moment, I could've argued that the real worry was mostly inside my head. I mean, the guy had said that weather might prevent him from reaching us. But now it was out in the open. I admitted to myself only then that I had kind of been looking to the Mountain Woman as a barometer of the threat we faced.

Our options were limited. We weren't in the cellular tax bracket, not that there'd be reception out here, anyway. By 6:40, I was at the Coleman cookstove, working on some "Organic Rice Pilaf with Raisins" while JM continued trying to read Mako's thought process from the wood fire. Hers was a distance mind-meld that was proving considerably more difficult than our earlier interspecies communion with the porpoises.

"Don't use that butter," JM called to me as I was wondering who we possibly could have told who wasn't as locked into Homer O'clock as Mako, or more so. The Bush Lines aren't exactly Swiss time.

"Why not?" I asked.

"We can use it to rub around in the trail mix as bait when we build our bird trap," she said matter-of-factly, snapping a piece of kindling over her thigh.

This is, in Alaska, the kind of woman they call "Good Breeding Stock."

By now all her comments just made me realize how serious the situation might be.

"JM?" I asked, stirring the pilaf.

"Hmm?"

"If it came to it, who do you think should be eaten first?"

"We could draw straws."

While thinking it over there in Halibut Cove, we both started to hum the 1970s Budweiser holiday Clydesdale jingle that had been implanted in my head twenty years earlier. I had taught it to JM on the trail.

"I could go for some pizza," JM finally said over the tasteless pilaf, as though in torturing ourselves life would bear a resemblance to its normal state.

* * * * *

We listened to the silence for a few minutes. It was pushing 7:00 P.M. and the atmosphere in the cabin was heavy but calm. Mako was now nine hours late, and I never felt so unsafe in a shelter. Starving takes a long time. I shivered when I imagined what would have happened if we hadn't found an unlocked cabin.

"Do you think we should start rationing?" I asked, with a mouth full of Polysorbate 80.

Surviving on Polysorbate 80

"Everything except the chocolate," JM said scientifically. "That isn't real energy."

"Chocolate? What chocolate?"

"I brought some of those Lindt truffles you like," she informed me, blowing into the gasping wood fire in the stove. "And there's chocolate in the trail mix that the birds won't like."

At my cabin JM almost never worked the fire. Was this a sign that some shift in her emotional state was taking place? Was she preparing for survival in the event that I died? JM, of course, was the Mountain Person here. I started watching her carefully to see if she was planning on cutting her losses and extending her supplies. At the same time, I was learning a thing or two by watching her method of getting a wet fire to catch: keep the door slightly open and blow from below.

For those who may be wondering, there were only two other discernible manifestations of Seasonal Affective Disorder (or, SAD, formerly Cabin Fever) I took note of in myself that first winter. One was a gloating op-ed piece I sent to the *Washington Post* regarding the lack of substantive effect even the worst Y2K scenario would have on my new rural life, and the other was about seven months of disoriented catatonia. The *Post* letter was politely turned down by an editor whom I often work with, probably with a mental note to encourage me to focus on safer topics, like war in Tajikistan.

Laying out all our food on the cabin table, we decided that we would eat the packaged pasta and processed rice complex carbos as normal, one a day for dinner until they were gone in four days. Then we'd move on to one cup of sodium soup mix and one piece of jerky each a day, and one oatmeal-with-raisins packet for breakfast. With that regimen, we could survive three weeks. JM, once a metabolism minor or something, explained the physiology of hunger as we rationed our preservative-laden board, which was suddenly looking as though it were comprised of precious, well-prepared delicacies.

"If you're putting in less than five hundred calories a day, your body automatically switches to starvation mode, and won't eat away at your stomach and other organs, for like a month. It's why starvation diets don't work at first. You also don't produce acne."

For a few moments I felt pleasantly surprised to find I had been loaded with so many standard features. It was like discovering a twenty dollar bill in one's coat pocket. Then the reality suddenly hit me, the way reality sometimes does, that no one besides Mako would likely come to this site again for four or five months. Three weeks' worth of food was worse than useless: it was torture.

* * * * *

The hours between 7:00 and 9:00 P.M. operated according to a two-part sequence. The casual observer would mostly hear nothing, but perhaps sense a more heightened . . . focus than is common across the bay. Then, every twenty-five minutes, a sublime wilderness pause would be punctured with JM saying something like, "He has to come tomorrow, right? I think he just gave himself a weather out and took it. Don't you think?"

And I'd say something analytical like, "You mean because of that 'I can usually get here usually' exchange?"

"Yes."

I would then look out the window at the lagoon. "But it's incredibly calm here."

"It's been snowing nonstop. And we don't know what the weather is in Homer. Or the wind."

During the 8:15 exchange, we both edged to the wall. Through the lagoonside window we examined the darkened horizon as though a minor emergency had elevated us in knowledge from our marine weather ignorance of forty-eight hours earlier. A murre swam sarcastically by below the cabin. We watched the water lap against the snowy bank for ten minutes. The porpoises were nowhere to be seen, which eliminated their backs as an escape route. Now we had fifteen minutes before JM's next hypothesis regarding our water-taxi driver.

It was a surreal situation: we weren't necessarily at the mercy of Big Bad Mother Nature. This could be, as JM had recognized, essentially a human problem, not a wilderness one. And if so, like so many twentieth-century life threats for the Western *Homo sapiens,* it was a preventable one. I tried to picture Mako's face, but couldn't. It was an Alaskan face—weather-beaten and irregularly shaven—which as far as I could tell left California when people were still saying, "Dude."

Whatever the cause of our situation, after our second evening's dinner it occurred to me that even if I one day looked back from my thermostat-heated, carbon monoxide-free split-level home and real-ized that excursions like this were just, for me, a lark, I for a time at least understood about assembling one of the basics of my life: I was respon-sible for my warmth. If I could just survive this quagmire, I thought, I could survive no matter where I was.

Small comfort. By 10:30 P.M. I couldn't stand it anymore. I started a discussion about splitting up for efficiency as I dumped an armload of split wood on the soaked cabin floor. "I could find the ranger station and the fictitious communications equipment and you could wait here for Mako," I announced to JM amidst a dusting of snow. I must've looked impressive there, dripping in my boxers with my peeled down waders.

JM's reply was instant. She didn't like the idea, and I didn't like her reason. "What if you flounder or get hurt?" she posited, probably thinking of my several wipeouts in the previous thirty-six hours alone. "I won't be there to help you." She felt sticking together was the only course to follow.

She, it turns out, had been formulating her own plans. "Which way is the community at Halibut Cove?" JM isn't very good with directions. It was one of the few practical areas of which I was in charge in our relationship.

"Around the lagoon bend toward the west here," I said, pointing across the deck, which was about equally wet and now about equally warm as the cabin.

"Could we walk?"

"As well as we could walk on the trail today," I said, making quotation marks with my fingers—an inexcusable felony—at the word "walk." Upon reflection, I thought that the populated part of the cove might be on an island, but I didn't mention it to JM. Instead I asked, "Do you really want to give up our water and fire here, where we are supposed to be picked up?"

That idea abandoned, I was for some reason still milking a determination to stay on plan. "If Mako doesn't come tomorrow, we should be able to get to the lake," I said, side-stepping the more obvious mini-lakes on the floor at about 11:15.

JM, from her tone not so sure that was wise, still wasn't ready to be the first one to explicitly abandon our skating mission. "Sounds good," she said evenly. Then after a pause she continued. "Although the tide gets later each day, so we'll have to wait longer for him, which means we'll have less and less daylight in which to forge ahead." JM has impeccable grammar. Slang on her lips sounds about as natural as a Torah reading by Louis Farrakhan.

We left it at that, and prepared to crash for an unexpected second night across the bay. Sometime after 12:30, JM's breathing took on the regularity of sleep. I was still brooding in my sleeping bag, Swiss chocolate flowing through my veins, when I remembered Sunny.

I sat up abruptly. JM asked me what was wrong, and we shifted into crisis mode. Code Red. Skating was out. If Mako didn't show the next day, I or we had to break into the ranger station and make use of whatever was there. If insufficient, we would have to fall back on my auxiliary plan to set the entire forest on fire to attract attention. I had brought enough Coleman fuel for just such a contingency.

Surviving on Polysorbate 80

I hoped I didn't have to implement the plan, which I could see as having expensive consequences. But I was aware we might not have any choice. Whereas before the whole experience had merely been about our own looming starvation, now it involved family. Here I was with plenty of warmth and, most significantly, access to the restroom facilities known as the woods. What Sunny wouldn't give for that right now, I reflected guiltily. Officially, this excursion was no longer within my Comfort Zone.

The expedition was only supposed to have been one day, 10 A.M. to 10 A.M. I'd planned to be back to let my dog out in the morning. Now it was already almost two days. She had plenty of food, of course. For a week at least. But if we were truly stranded, even Sunny would eventually get hungry.

JM tried to steady me with conversation. "Well, if Mako comes I'm off jerky for a while," she commented while I stood vigil by the window.

"As soon as I see his boat approaching, I'll start eating every one of those beef hearts. I'll eat all 80 Polysorbates." One night of food rationing was proving a challenge for me.

If there was a positive side effect of the resulting anxiety, it was that I finally motored through an epochal Wallace Stegner novel that had been bogging me down for months. Eventually JM and I fell into a dank, uneasy sleep, dreaming, we conferred later, of cannibalism and starving dogs.

* * * * *

The engine sound was so much like I expected it to be, I just treated it like another aural mirage and continued brooding on the deck. "We should sign the guest registry," JM said in a very Relaxed Tone as the orange and blue Whaler grew undeniably larger in the lagoon. It was 11:15 A.M., Wednesday, December 16, Trip Day Three, more than twenty-five hours after pickup time. With her statement, we decided to downplay the fact that we had essentially been weeping inside for much of the previous day. That was to stay between us for a while. The decision had been made by Mako: we were to live. It's not too often someone makes that kind of decision for you without realizing it.

"I don't know if that's wise," I replied. "They might track us down. We're technically in for $100 to the State of Alaska, or Exxon/Mobil, or whoever controls this place."

But then I had a last-second change of heart and I hastily jotted the following down next to comments such as "Great place!" "Thanks!" and "Saw Lots of Bears!" signed by people from places like Munich and Toronto while JM swept out the cabin:

December, if you follow the Gregorian Calendar:

Forced to eat my limbs in an attempt to generate enough energy to complete plan of cattle liberation. Blood flowing uncontrollably, which is why you may find the floor wet. But discovered it (blood) is also an effective fire starter. Hangnails make good dental floss. Ran out of ganja on Day Sixteen. Watched porpoises.

—Jack London

JM had to remind me, but I kept my middle-of-the-night, prematurely starving jerky-binging promise. It took Mako ten minutes to reach us, and a lot can be ingested, if not digested, in ten minutes. I thus didn't enjoy the ride back, although it seemed much shorter than the ride out. I couldn't help noticing it had stopped snowing. The water was now a flat mild aqua which, were it not for the incongruity of visible glaciers, could be equitably compared to some of the more calm shelves of the Caribbean.

"Thought I'd forgotten you, eh, dude?" Mako asked as he moored. He was wearing standard Mountain Man-issue work coveralls.

"Ha," I snorted casually. "What was the delay? Weather?"

"Dude died on the bay yesterday," he Free Ranged by way of confirmation. "A Russian. Boat flipped on him. I still tried to come out to get you, but friends came down and stopped me. Twice."

JM made the appropriate grunts of appreciation while I flung our packs onto the boat. In my pocket I felt the paper clip we had found in the cabin we were going to fashion into a fishhook. I thought to ask Mako if anyone had made a film version of Robinson Crusoe, but decided the Mountain Manly thing to do was to let it go. It hadn't been his fault.

"We're at war," Mako said as he gunned us past the porpoises, who had returned to the lagoon to say good-bye. On past trips I had always asked upon pickup what was going on in the world, in case there was some horrible deadline I had waiting for me on my answering machine. Mako was used to it, and this time preempted me. "Or soon will be. I'm not sure if they inserted the quarter into the video game yet. Quarter of a trillion that is."

"Pyongyang?" JM guessed. "Sudan?"

"Nothing so clever. Just Iraq," Mako said in a disappointed tone. "Also they're impeaching the President. There are some who think these two events are not unrelated."

"President of Exxon?" I asked.

"Nope. President of Cameroon, dude," Mako said, accepting the half a Polysorbate 80 stick I passed him. "Did you have fun? Did you skate? Was it cold out there?"

I may have answered that everything "went fine." Maybe it was the sudden absence of overwhelming silence, but I was distracted. I didn't realize how loud that silence had been, or the degree to which Homer, even innocently, represented civilization. I also had occasion to note a brief, nagging sensation that I had missed something. It was getting cluttered up behind all those "happy to be alive" endorphins. But it had to do with a pristine turquoise pond. A dense quiet. And ice skating.

✷ ✷ ✷ ✷ ✷

The sun was almost tauntingly circular and bright above the spit as we loaded the Subaru. JM and I were in a condition known as Driving While Happy as we headed back through town. It was lucky we weren't pulled over. DWH kills many Alaskans every year: conventions like "right side of the street" and "minimum speed limits" feel arbitrary. Every snowshoe hare deserves examination, immediately. It's like letting four-year-olds get behind the wheel. One day, mark my words, there will be laws against being so emotionally together in a moving vehicle. DWH is most commonly caused by leaving all of society's inputs for at least forty-eight hours.

It sometimes takes the contrast of town life to make one realize one is under the influence of rural happiness. A friend once pointed out that even the ravens in town seem to possess a frenetic neurosis not shared by their more rural cousins.

And so we were ripe to be jolted by life after the other side of the bay. KBBI said it was six degrees in downtown Homer. Bombs were exploding in Baghdad. NPR pundits were analyzing them via satellite. "We did use the B-2 bomber for the first time in the second sortie, Noah," I thought I heard one of them say, from Pentagon Media Headquarters in Virginia.

At this point as we drove home, I was thinking that somewhere between the real danger of Alaskan winter wilderness and my own goofy lack of preparation lies the rural Cheechako survival experience. Snowy conditions exist. There is real danger out there, even at the dawn of the twenty-first century. We could have been better prepared. We could have informed friends more explicitly of our dates. We could even have let the state park people know. Or we could've waited several years until we owned a boat and understood the bay. Or we could've brought real shovels, or a gun. Or at least a compass. But we didn't, and that, for me, is part of the Mountain Man learning curve.

I have never once regretted not owning a cellular phone, which would bring me another step closer to the side of natural selection on which I don't want to be. The side likely to be composed of people who'll

Surviving on Polysorbate 80

survive about a day if it all comes crashing down. Until then, it would change the game, like bringing a knife into a boxing match, or snowmachining the Iditarod. It would exercise different muscles.

But I did hear an unnerving report on the Alaska Public Radio Network's *Alaska News Nightly* program not long after we returned: a family of hunters, these folks with cell phones and radio equipment, got stuck more than a week extra in the wilderness somewhere in Southeast Alaska at about the same time we were in the Kachemak Bay backcountry. Even though they were warm and in constant contact, the National Guard had flown two food dropoffs to them, until the weather finally cleared enough for them to be rescued. Slackers. Had they not heard of Polysorbate 80? It is incredibly portable. Basically what I learned from the report was that a cellular phone entitles you to free take-out delivery on the taxpayers.

When the news spot finished, I wondered if this surprising new attitude of mine, created largely by our previous two days, indicated approaching Mountain Manhood. In one regard, probably: I was learning to scoff at the tourists.

* * * * *

Sunny was amazing. She spent the extra day engaged in a thorough investigation of the garbage, but there was plenty of food left. Because of a subliminal knowledge about the best laid plans of Homer O'clock, I had laid out newspapers on the kitchen floor for the first time since she was a tiny puppy, eight years earlier. And she used them. As I cleaned up the newspapers, I related the adventure across the bay to her in a very Relaxed Tone.

She acted interested. Or at least, she held no grudge. In fact, she seemed delighted to see the shaggy guy who passed out the peanut butter biscuits with regularity. We rolled and bit each other in the snow beside the deck.

A few days later, it was winter solstice. After a long, fiery sauna at JM's to roast all the Polysorbate 80 out of my system, we went skating at midnight on the frozen groomed tennis court behind the old Homer middle school. I had my hockey equipment. There were shooting stars and a lime shimmer of aurora. We could hear the bay crashing in loping crescendos along the shore in the darkness, and every now and then a diesel rig driving by on the road to Anchorage.

Step Two: Food

But the missionary was a bother after all, for he brought no

meat into the camp, and he ate heartily, and the hunters

grumbled. But he chilled his lungs on the divide by the Mayo,

and the dogs afterwards nosed the stones away and

fought over his bones.

—Jack London, *The Law of Life*

Chapter 5
Pack Ice Driver's Ed

*I*t had been a long, hard winter. By any standards. I discerned this from Roger muttering into his bar coaster about the "darn global cooling" phenomenon. Actually, I could tell on my own. There had been signs. Like when my toilet exploded one morning in January. Temperatures hadn't been above zero for eleven days. Astonished old-timers said Kachemak Bay hadn't frozen like this in half a century.

Restroom facilities in the twelve-foot snowdrift off my deck proved inconvenient following my toilet's demolition, not to mention unsanitary and a bit unsafe. I was sharing my outhouse with a starving moose, who charged me every time I headed toward it. I knew how she felt. The winter of 1998–99 was frustrating for everyone. I returned from these daily adventures with frosted eyebrows.

When spring finally sprang in May, I rubbed my eyes, emerged from semi-hibernation, and almost immediately started having Step Two thoughts.

I wasn't sure that I had dispatched with Step One during the agonizing months after being rescued from Mako by Mako. In fact on the day of the first thaw I noticed that the ceiling above my bed now bowed almost deferentially in a two-foot bubble, the result of my inability to master the engineering skills required to remove eight feet of snow from my roof. But I gradually and with some frostbite came to reconcile this minor architectural mishap by arguing that there is only so much cold a warm-blooded creature can investigate in a chilly world.

"Survive much?" Laura asked me from the General Store on May 7 when I told her about my near roof cave-in just as the first green became visible around Fritz Creek. Madly flipping letters into people's postal boxes, she was as unstoppably frenetic as all Alaskans are when the sun starts to wake us again.

"Hey, I was as waterless as you were for four months," I protested, a little hurt. I had expected my standing among my neighbors to improve when I acquired the merit badge of frozen pipes that had me melting snow on the stove from January through April. I was disappointed by the results of my only slightly Free Ranged accounts of near freezings.

Just a week earlier, my well water had burst back into liquid state in a geyser through my *Where the Wild Things Are* poster. This had sent me flying outside at 5:14 A.M., naked but for waders, to shut off the main water valve to the cabin. Laura knew this. Not having a well at her place, she was pointedly unimpressed.

"Yes, but you had expectations of water, and therefore suffer needlessly," Laura replied, in a tone nature documentary narrators use to say things like, "The dry season is long and brutal for the wildebeest."

"This is what I've been trying to explain to you," Laura said. She is thin and petite, but she has a commanding presence that I estimated began when she was about three years old.

We bantered about the Balkans for a few minutes as I addressed some letters. As we chatted, we felt our solar batteries recharging and danced in place to the rhythm of actual moving electrons in our cells. We were humans without melanin, blinking like moles at the new sunlight. Then Laura passed me some postage and, probably as an excuse to get out into the sunshine, asked me casually if I would mind helping her change the carburetor pin in her truck parked in front of the store.

I froze. Old memories of not being able to Do Things came rushing back at me, and my smile started to melt. I am not one of the strange specialists who understands the workings of the internal combustion engine. Better not try to Free Range, I thought. I might get her killed.

"Um. Not only can I not identify a carburetor," I disclosed out loud. "I'm not sure I know what a carburetor is. It's where the fuel mixes with air, right?"

"Survive much?" she inquired again, handing me my change.

On the radio, the DJ was listing statewide temperatures as though they were the latest life expectancy figures. My good spirits returned, and I flashed a smile at Laura. I suddenly felt it was okay, the piece-by-piece pace at which I was trying to ascend from Cheechakohood. Each new confession of incompetence allowed me to fill in another piece of the puzzle. There was no need to deny reality.

"Hey, if only my clan had survived, humans would just now be inventing clothes," I explained. "And only if we lived up here in February when the stove wasn't going." We both looked out the window and sighed at the budding alder. The whole world stank of chlorophyll.

Such unabashed honesty was purifying, but the conversation with Laura briefly set me to thinking about the value of mechanical knowledge in remote rural conditions. Especially when my car broke down not fifteen minutes after I left the General Store. It occurred to me that I should probably start asking the Rogers of the world if I might watch them as they repaired their trucks and stuff. But engine maintenance didn't feel like a high priority, not in this weather. It wasn't as though this gap in my Cheechako education could prove fatal. "Look at the situation I'm faced with now," I reasoned. "I just need to wait for the tow truck."

I had other thoughts on my mind anyway. Namely, Step Two thoughts. They had been dancing around my head now for a week. I think because I had all winter to realize the value of stocking up on food before winter. But I remember the date of that latest Cheechako-exposing chat with Laura and the car trouble that followed, not only because it was the afternoon the devil's club started sprouting their pistachio ice cream scoop buds, but also because it was the day I first got the message to study subsistence from the experts. As soon as possible.

* * * * *

Pack Ice Driver's Ed

I can even pinpoint the moment my acute Step Two pursuit launch occurred. It happened during the fourth hour I was stuck in the clutch-frying mud bog above my driveway on my way home from the exchange with Laura. In Fritz Creek it was the height of breakup, Alaska's name for spring, or the transformation of everyone and everything into mud molecules.

The biggest catalyst was simply that my afternoon-long wait for the Homer O'clock tow truck was making me hungry. I couldn't run down to the cabin for a quick lunch of local halibut, because if the tow truck waded in during the interim, I would miss what I knew was my only chance for rescue. Every third clutch, strut, and transmission was fried on the Kenai Peninsula during breakup. It wasn't anyone's fault. Except maybe the mud's. So I waited.

And waited.

It could be days. I realized this. Mako, in even agreeing to schedule a specific day of appointment, represents the pinnacle of Homer O'clock customer service. Moose and grouse were trotting by as I crouched in a haze of rancid clutch smoke, and there was nothing I could do about it. I watched as probably a half dozen of each cantered by me wearing what looked like smirks. This kind of situational torture can firm a resolution in a fellow's mind. My stomach rumbled so loudly that Sunny, sitting in the mud next to me, growled at it. This was it: I was in pursuit of Step Two.

"Forget about internal combustion engines," I murmured to myself. "Food gathering is the next task for me."

A week later, on May 15, I found myself on a plane heading 960 miles north, to the top of the North American continent. I was going so far up, I was almost going down. My goal was the Iñupiat town of Barrow, on the Arctic Ocean, for the spring whale harvest.

This seemed to be the sensible place for Lesson One in Step Two. On Alaska's North Slope, there were folks who had proven pretty good at Step Two for at least the past several thousand years. What I particularly wanted to learn first was what you did when you actually caught your own meal: how did you carve it up and get it to the table? I had a feeling it was not very much like a trip to the local Safeway meat counter. If I mastered whale butchering, I imagined, carving a mere moose back in Fritz Creek should be a piece of cake.

Fantasy had once again played its part in my decision to make this trip. While I had sat famished on my disabled Subaru's bumper for what turned out to be six hours, I had quite clearly seen myself astride the back of one of the forty-ton bowheads that many Northern Alaskans fancy. It's what's for dinner. I had myself scouring for icebergs while the ulus sliced. Some versions saw me clutching the blowhole for balance.

✶ ✶ ✶ ✶ ✶

Instead here I was, on my third morning in Barrow, frightfully, unforgivably delaying an entire family of subsistence whale hunters from performing its by-definition most important subsistence task. Why? Because I was waiting for my rental snowmachine to show up on the ice beach below the family's house, just as I had waited for my tow truck barely a week earlier in Fritz Creek. I could almost hear Laura guffawing.

The extended members of the Leavitt family were ready to go. They were as politely as possible pawing the ground from atop their snowmachines and behind their wooden sleds. The rearmost sleds contained the elders and the Pepsi cans that glinted in the bashful sun so close to magnetic north that the satellite dishes that recently transformed the community of Barrow from mere Dynasty reruns to fully Geraldo-ized point down toward the ground.

By simply boarding an Alaska Airlines flight, I had earned myself a state of stress above the 71st parallel that the morning commuter in Houston might recognize. Here they were, this Eskimo clan, about to head out on the 3,006th annual spring bowhead whale harvest (except

Pack Ice Driver's Ed

for the moratorium year of 1977 and one year in the mid-500s when the captain overslept), and a shaggy Cheechako was holding them up. I saw it as a touchy situation there at 7:00 A.M. on May 17, ten days after my clutch fried, and one hour after I had been invited to participate in a Step Two spectacle unparalleled in the human experience: the butchering of an animal that would feed an entire community.

I was incredibly lucky to have been asked along. And the opportunity was in danger of slipping through my fingers. That wasn't all. When your family's whaling crew strikes a bowhead, you don't sit around. You blaze out to whale camp and bring it to shore. Immediately. Freshness is the key. Whales come with no preservatives.

Given that I had been included at the last minute by their matriarch to join the Leavitts for their journey to whale camp, I was becoming more than a little concerned about the social faux pas I might be committing in delaying the whole operation, not to mention the regionwide famine for which I might be responsible. I was becoming so concerned, in fact, that a tingly nervousness was giving me pinprick shocks all over my body to mark each second that the snowmachine I had booked continued not to show up at our appointed spot. The pinpricks had an almost magnetic quality, and increased in intensity so rapidly that it occurred to me that I might actually be part of the planet's pending polar reversal.

I'd been reading up on the phenomenon ever since I got the Subaru unstuck in Fritz Creek. They say the Earth's magnetic poles are due for their regular exchange some time in the next few hundred thousand years, and I was feeling all kinds of evidence in the behavior inspired in myself and those who lived here that the switch might soon be upon us. Any millennium now.

Vehicle-less in the Leavitt's backyard, I had a vision of this reversal as taking place in all the axes, not just space. For instance, take the time axis. A snowmachine supposedly arriving for me below the Leavitt house bluff "within fifteen minutes" could be imminently reversed to mean, "Fifteen minutes prior to the Apocalypse." You see? Just invert everything. Ideas. Space. Time. I thought I might be living the opposite day that kids play. I even had my sweater on backward.

I'd felt the hint of transitional polar pull since the moment I arrived two days earlier in a temporary thinning of fog, which the airline industry has long since learned to pounce on with fast-motion boarding, pull-back, and take-off before you've stashed your extra carry-on bag.

Though it was constantly on my mind, I couldn't dwell coherently on the implications of polar reversal at the moment. I needed my snowmachine to show up while the Leavitts were still hanging out in their yard, as I didn't exactly know my way around the local trails. Only by traveling with the family would I find its whale camp amidst hundreds of square miles of monolithic ice. This is even harder than getting around Boston. Tricky enough even as polar magnetism stands now. Directions are hard to give on pack ice. I mean, what was someone supposed to say? "Turn left at the seventy-ninth ice bump?"

The Leavitts didn't seem overly concerned about polar reversal. Or even about me and the delay I was causing. Few of the people milling about on the ice, revving their snowmachines, or loading their sleds even seemed to notice me. Since my inclusion had come at such a late hour, there had been no time for most of the family to be briefed about my presence. And yet everyone seemed to accept that we were all waiting for one more snowmachine to arrive.

"Why don't you come in the sled?" a friendly young woman in her early twenties who had no idea what I was doing on the ice in front of her home finally asked me after thirty minutes of this tingly unease. But I couldn't help noticing that there was nobody between the ages of three and eighty in any of the sleds, and I felt climbing in might hurt my profile as a hunter. These conveyances were the ones dog teams used to pull before it became clear how much easier a 120-horsepower engine is to feed.

"I'll be along soon," I said, idiotically gazing sideways as if at something in about two hundred miles of pure pack ice. "I have that snowmachine coming. You guys go on without me."

The young woman, who I would learn was named Marylou, was a daughter of the vacationing yet nonetheless heroic and successful whaling captain Oliver Leavitt. She shrugged, made a slight hand gesture, and the caravan began to glide off toward the "horizon," which was all but the whole world: a ghostly shimmering two-tone universe of solid gray ceiling and white floor which had settled in to coincide at fifty feet like a jaw closing, about thirteen seconds after I landed in Barrow.

The trail I wished I was on, a faint indentation in the white extending from the sleds ahead of me, set off vaguely south and west-ish through this limited spectrum. But this is only an educated guess, as pretty much every place on the planet is south of here, currently. This cuts down on directions by 25 percent. Once clear of downtown Barrow, the trail circled back north, toward a several-acre camp at the nebulous end of the continent along the Arctic Ocean, about eighteen miles away.

A girl of twelve turned around on her machine (Alaska requires no driver's license for snowmachines, whose speedometers go up to 130 miles per hour) and sort of smiled at me. Her eyes said, "Come along now, silly boy. This is your only chance. We all know that. Hop into a sled with my grandmother." I just waved again, stupidly.

The caravan line grew smaller like one of Mako's boats as it snaked away. Soon all I could hear was the wind, which was light by local standards, perhaps eighty miles per hour. Now it was pushing 7:15 A.M. Monday, almost exactly four hours after the Leavitt whaling crew had struck a bowhead. The family had been organized and was heading to camp to land it and carve it up.

I sighed. I'd heard there were people whose primary nutrition didn't come from a supermarket. I found this interesting. I was curious how the species *Homo sapiens* lived.

* * * * *

In two minutes, I wouldn't be able to see the caravan at all. Some more members of the Leavitt family were running out of the house fifteen yards above me, hopping on snowmachines beside the daypack at my feet, and zapping across the ice to catch the main bulk of the clan. I just didn't feel like I could delay them any more.

My big Step Two field opportunity had all started with a phone call I had received a little over an hour earlier, when I was sitting on my bed at the Top of the World Hotel in downtown Barrow, wondering how I was going to get out on the arctic ice pack and pick up some subsistence skills. I had made some inquiries back in Fritz Creek, but I was basically starting with few connections in Barrow. The call came while I sat watching A&E's Marilyn Monroe *Biography* within view of that vast sea of white. It was Maggie at the Alaska Eskimo Whaling Commission on the line, helpfully informing me of the Leavitt crew bowhead strike three hours earlier at 3:00 that morning. She suggested I call Captain Oliver's wife, Annie, to see if I might visit the Leavitt camp. That's where they do the harvesting. I made the call with great trepidation because I'd been told that an Icelandic documentary team had been trying for two and a half years to get out on the ice with a whaling crew.

"Sure, c'mon over, we're heading out to camp," Annie said offhandedly, then cupped the phone to yell an order at someone, before returning momentarily to me. "We're at Number 916 (all houses in Barrow are just identified by a number, regardless of street). Ever driven a snowmachine?"

"Well, um, for a little while the other day," I stammered, forgetting to Free Range. "Only it was one of those giant Cadillac-y ones that pretty much drives itself. But my girlfriend has driven them lots of times and she says it's really easy."

To my astonishment, that odd spontaneous tactic worked. This woman, who'd spent her entire life within 1,129 miles of the North Pole, was apparently unperturbed at my lack of ice cap experience. She said the same thing everyone had been saying to me about snowmachines since I moved to Alaska. "Ah, you'll probably be okay. You just press it and it goes. Brake when you want to stop. Do you have one?"

I just blurted, "How much time do I have?"

"Oh, thirty minutes." She was yelling orders to someone else before the phone clicked down.

Things, amazing things, just seem to happen so suddenly in Alaska. Just a week earlier I had been stuck in a mud bog with Sunny, fantasizing about Step Two. Now, at the Top of the World Hotel as soon as Annie hung up, I reflected that Homer O'clock for the Eskimo family of a crew that has just struck a whale is about as close to nuclear timepiece precision as noncorporate human beings get. This was the year's staple food. In 1999. There is no McDonalds' in Barrow, incidentally, but I saw on a bulletin board that someone flies in Happy Meals and sells them out of his house: would official economic figures represent fried grease as a Barrow "import"?

To understand the magnitude of a family striking a whale I only had to listen to the VHF radio band on which everyone communicates when a crew makes a strike.

"Hey hey hey hey!!" someone hollers. Followed by a stream of Inupiaq exclamations of joy and prayer that invariably includes, *Aarigaa:* sort of an "It's all good" life affirmation. Like an Eskimo *L'Chaiyim.*

So if Annie said thirty minutes, she probably meant, well, not more than an hour or two. This was still Alaska.

Thus began one of the great snowmachine rounding-up operations in recent North Slope memory. Barrow ranks with the friendliest places I've ever been in terms of locals trying to help you. The whale meat, which is divided according to a long-standing, extremely formalized and Karmic system that ensures few in the town go hungry, spawns a community mind. I don't think there were many people on the Slope who didn't know that a Cheechako *Tunnic* (Iñupiaq for non-Iñupiat) was looking for wheels, or tracks, or whatever you call it. People I had just met were calling neighbors and eavesdropping on scientific VHF radio channels for me to see if there were any machines available on the public dole.

Still, 6:15 A.M. on a Monday in Barrow is not one of your great business hours of operation. If someone's family or crew had struck a whale during these few weeks when the bowhead pods glided through (and many if not most of Barrow's fortyish crews had struck one; the season was going great), market economy "work" simply didn't happen. Whether it was at school, at the 8,000 North Slope Borough administration buildings, or at the one Barrow grocery store, it was whale time. If someone's family or crew hadn't harpooned (and then blown up with discharge bombs) a giant mammal, he or she wasn't awake yet.

Finally someone whose name I never got, and who I think was the long-cajoled brother of an executive of middle level at the Ukpeagvik Iñupiat Corporation (UIC), told me via the sleepy and overwhelmed switchboard operator at the Top of the World Hotel that he'd be on the ice below the Leavitt's bluff in fifteen minutes (he knew where to go: everyone knows everyone here).

I squished to #916 at top speed; Barrow, a polygon set on permafrost, not being one of your difficult-to-get-around towns. I don't choose the verb "squished" lightly, either. In Homer I had sprayed my boots just before leaving for the airport with anti-wetness toxin. Thus I continue to observe that the most wild places seem to bring me into my closest contact with the most polluting substances. In the perpetual surface goop of spring in Barrow, however, the stuff was proving hopelessly ineffective. The world was the consistency of tofu. My feet were soaked by the time I was ten steps out of the Top of the World's front door.

As I cross-sectioned Barrow, stomping past plywood shacks teetering right next to funky Alaskan Gothic geo-domes, I noticed that monster piles of *muktuk*—smooth jet-black whale skin attached to an inch or more of coconut-looking blubber—were already piling up in yards and on doorsteps, in preparation for storage in ice cellars cut out of the ground. It was a method I decided to keep in mind for when my energy-draining, Nixon-era Kelvinator finally moved on to fridge heaven.

* * * * *

I knew I had arrived at the Leavitts' because of the snowmachine derby chopping outside. I immediately liked Annie, who ran your basic middle-American arctic household. As soon as I puffed into her kitchen, in which old women who weren't speaking English were baking what looked and smelled remarkably like bagels, she started yelling at me for not dressing warmly enough.

I was the only non-Eskimo person I'd see for nineteen hours in an extremely social situation, and I was instantly being treated like family. I decided not to give her any lip. I pulled out my turquoise Space Age pants and started worming my way into them over my ripped Dockers trousers and my new hunting sword alongside the other kids on the Leavitt kitchen floor. People were tramping in and out. Not one seemed to think it odd that this shaggy-haired *Tunnic* born 7,000 miles away was sitting on their floor struggling with his plastic ankle snap.

When I was wearing all the clothes I had brought, I started outside, thanking Annie for the invite as I closed the door. She was staying behind for now as an HQ radio dispatch woman and chef. So far, so good. All I had to do was wait fifteen minutes for the snowmachine rental agent.

And twenty minutes after the fifteen minutes had passed, the cajoled UIC executive's brother still wasn't there with my snowmachine. And this was when the Leavitt caravan started to disappear into the horizon. And the pinpricks continued working their tingly way down my spine.

This next minute on the ice beach below the Leavitt's was one of the worst of my life. Far more horrible than the frustration of waiting for a Homer tow truck. The reverse polarization (or just stress-induced) tin-gling was getting worse. In fact, I was as tense as if I had been stuck in rush hour traffic. True, I was glad I had refused a sled ride and let the unbelievably welcoming family go and subsist without me, but had I done it soon enough? With every burst of Iñupiaq to emit from the Leavitt family VHF, which was sitting between me and the house, I imagined I translated, *The whale's gone. We brought it to shore, but we waited too long and it floated away along with several of the crew. What held you up?*

Seven seconds after one of these mirage translations, a floating dot actually did appear on the horizon. Five seconds after that, it seemed to be clearly headed for me. Three seconds later still, a sleepy, fuzzy-faced man with the aura of having an infant who had kept him up all night was telling me, "There's no key. Just start it up by yanking here. This switch is for (words immediately forgotten) and this one here is the hand warmer. This way on, this way off. Don't ever open the choke: it floods right up. Even if you're stopped for five hours and the engine's cold, just keep pulling the cord until it starts."

I wondered if "choking" a snowmachine engine was the same as "priming" a chainsaw engine. As I had learned from the carburetor pin exchange with Laura, I should've taken shop in school. I was only half able to pay attention to the lecture proper because the last stragglers of the Leavitt family were disappearing down the forty-five-foot bluff face from the house and snaking away up the pack ice. One had just jogged out of the front door and grabbed the radio. These people were my last hope of catching the caravan and finding the whale camp.

The first thing I noticed on my prospective vehicle, after the gaping hole where the ignition key belonged, was the saddle-shaped swath of duct tape under the rental agent across what had once been the seat. That and a small jagged triangle of Plexiglas in the lower right-hand corner of the dash which before the most recent crash possibly had been the windscreen. "This machine's in really sweet shape," the UIC executive's brother had told me on the phone.

Suddenly I observed that my worries were very different from what they had been when I was merely writhing over holding up the whole whaling expedition. Now my problem was that I had to figure out how to drive the kind of conveyance that makes the Alaskan obituary pages read like a snowmachine clinic. On the fly. This was a new and troubling development. It reminded me of the How Good I Had It A Moment Ago Syndrome that I had first noticed during Chainsawgate. This syndrome always makes me feel dumb for not being satisfied with the usually safer condition of things a moment ago.

"Hold your tongue," I said to Laura, who was a thousand miles south. This snowmachine didn't look like it would hold together for a mile. Then a thought hit me: had she been trying to warn me about just this kind of situation with her carburetor pin request?

"Um," I said to the rental agent, pointing to the chopping vehicle. "It's just that . . . well, one question: how do you, you know, operate it?"

The UIC executive's brother looked at me for a full three seconds unblinkingly. Then he pointed to the handlebar and gave me that piece of pack ice advice more useful than any driver's ed course offered anywhere in the world: "This makes it go. This makes it stop." He said this in a totally flat voice, like a New Yorker might explain a Walk/Don't Walk sign.

The last thing the rental agent imparted to me as he hopped off the still-running machine and presented it palms open like a game show hostess, was, "You know, so just drive it carefully."

I said, "I will. I'm an excellent snowmachine driver" in my best Rain Man voice. I pulled on my Subcomandante Marcos mask and threw one turquoise leg over the seat.

Then I accidentally grazed the throttle and the thing jumped. I left my skin there, talking with the UIC executive's brother about snowmachine safety, while my soul rebounded like a sling shot toward the Arctic Ocean and the end of North America.

* * * * *

The drive was eighteen miles, 12,000 years. The straightaway part of the trail, tracing the iceline a few miles inland, was basically four-foot ridges bracketed by sinkholes (ideal for say, ice fishing, or disappearing Cheechakos). I was terrified of the machine, of course, gripping it until my knuckles were white as I hurtled over notched turquoise undulations with the knees-jutted-out body language one usually sees in motorcross psychotics. It is truly scary to anticipate landing after hitting air in a snowmachine, which is a vehicle that makes the Ford Pinto seem well-engineered. No matter how much I braced myself for the impact, I always smashed into the ground with a lopsided force that shocked me, and caused the steering column to greet my belly intimately.

After about three seconds, I wasn't even trying to catch up to the Leavitt caravan anymore. I was just trying to stay on my vehicle. The snow-machine was just insanely fast. It appeared to know no other pace. Through no choice of my own, then, I soon reached the family, whose rear members looked back at me with indefinable expressions and sort of nodded. I was the only one fighting for control and weaving over the dangerously hollow ice in a reckless manner that would've concerned me a week before if I had seen my neighbor's kids exhibiting such behavior on their ATVs.

Barrow disappeared shockingly quickly behind us as I discovered and experimented with this "brake" mechanism my rental agent had so effectively explained. A narrow parallelogram of actual nonfoggy world—jagged at the edges like a battleship with turrets—was visible toward the slowly expanding northern horizon. It was the first significant break in the gray-white universe I had seen since arriving above the Arctic Circle. In fact, the sun-diffusing ceiling around Barrow had lifted to an almost unheard-of high of three inches of the haunting storm blue that seemed to lurk underneath every cloud layer up there.

It proved a temporary and periodic unveiling, which almost made me weep, as on my flight up I had observed an Alaska-wide map in the newspaper that pictorially displayed climactic conditions across the whole state. Giant smiling suns had been plastered literally everywhere in Alaska except Barrow. Homer was looking at sixty degrees and clear—and I had left. I sighed at the memory of all that beautiful mud.

By 7:45 A.M., I had learned the many benefits of the brake mechanism. I was soon glad for the slow pace of the caravan necessitated by the cargo, which included what looked like some heavy mechanical equipment. I was glad because I had lost my new, already scratched $10 rose-tinted sunglasses sometime Sunday "night" in Barrow (the sun wouldn't set again until August 2 around America's northernmost city). The result was fourteen hours later, in the back of the Leavitt caravan, I fought through the already misty world—allowing in the best of circumstances a few dozen feet of visibility—with eyes fogged by a constant pool of wind-generated tears. With no windscreen to speak of on my snowmachine, I needed wipers on my eyes.

With what remained of my vision, I noticed the fuel gauge was flapping wildly between "1/4" and "E" on the display panel. It crossed my mind to inquire what kind of gas mileage snowmachines get. I could tell neither how fast nor how far we were traveling, because neither the speedometer needle nor the odometer counter moved at all.

* * * * *

In Alaska, you can be both warm and cold at the same time. My extremities felt fine at this early part of the day Monday, but around two miles from Barrow I considered pulling the Marcos hat down completely over my eyes to prevent the stinging from the tiny ice shards that flew in uneven dashes from the snowmachine tracks and made the world look like a very old movie. I abandoned this line of thinking because I felt it might have an adverse effect on my steering.

Just then, at perhaps 7:55 A.M., although I was deafened by the snowmachine's engine noise, I discerned from the body language on the sled ahead of me that the mood was changing from back-slapping kidding around to arms-aloft jubilation. Soon I saw why. A figure was riding toward us out of the pack ice holding up a flag. The banner was sort of like a military standard, yet the figure somehow carried it in a relaxed manner more evocative of, say, a Capture the Flag game.

We all stopped as quickly as the ice allowed and I watched as a solid young woman named Loyala leaped off a snowmachine next to mine. She started hopping expectantly up and down. With no one gunning an engine for a moment, I could hear her boots crunching in the shadow-tinged ice. The approaching rider looked to be a member of the Leavitt whaling crew that had brought down the bowhead early that morning.

"Hey hey hey hey!!" everyone yelled. I thrust my arms up in the air, too, yelling, *"Mazel Tov!"* Not much of a public high-fiver, I immediately looked around self-consciously after my pep squad gesture, but then reflected, "That's pretty amazing: catching a whale. How many whales could Mark McGuire catch in a season?"

The standard bearer set down his flag and strutted over like . . . like, some kind of hunter after a successful kill. He was a young man, in his mid-twenties, stubbled, wearing a gory, once-white, fur-lined parka, and metal aviator sunglasses—an indigenous Mod fashion statement, by all accounts. I recognized the look on his face—I've worn the same joyous, satisfied, primeval hunter expression when I've pulled a salmon from a stream on a fishing trip.

Loyala ran over toward the solitary snowmachine and embraced its driver in one of those Armistice postures of leg-bent formalized passion before the man, who was miming a quick rundown of the hunt, let himself be kissed by all the relatives. He was beaming, glowing. Everyone was. This was the zenith. Personally, family-wise, culturally, the moment everyone had been waiting for. Step Two: mission accomplished.

Skipping back to her machine, Loyala uttered her first words to me: "That's my boyfriend, Billy. His dad Oliver's the captain. He shot the whale with his harpoon. Why don't you kill your engine when we stop?"

"There's no key," I explained, blinking away wind tears. "I'm concerned it won't start up again. Congratulations on the whale."

She seemed to accept that, and the caravan began to move off again. When I hopped back on my own snowmachine, I felt the near-gutting from the sword inside my Space Age pants that was becoming so familiar on the North Slope of Alaska. I had known in advance to bring a "hunting knife" to the polar sphere (the way you bring a towel to beaches in the tropics) because of the Ice Safety Guidelines the Alaska Eskimo Whaling Commission had faxed me when I had first made inquiries about learning Step Two from what can only be called the pros.

I guess I had gotten a little carried away with the Step Two spirit in my purchase at Ulmer's Hardware. The thing was medieval militia gear. The knife is officially intended for use when you fall through the global-warmed pack ice. You're supposed to jam the blade into the wall of the hole into which you've slipped. And proceed to pray for rescue.

From my seat, I made some notes connecting ice integrity and sunglass possession to breeding success 330 miles above the Arctic Circle. Evidently more notes than I had intended. When I looked up, I had a moment of panic. The Leavitt snowmachines and sleds were a wavering darker dot on the vast white before me. They were so far away I couldn't even see them advancing any more. They seemed to be jogging in space.

On a related issue, despite racking my brains, I couldn't for the life of me remember what Paragraph Eight, Subsections A through E, of the Alaska Eskimo Whaling Commission Guidelines, Polar Bears Section, suggested if you encounter a polar bear on a 120-horsepower vehicle. I consulted the top end of the nonfunctional speedometer. I wasn't confident that even that velocity was faster than a lean, in-shape ursine quadruped could hightail it, especially if the wind was with him or her. I wondered if the Polysorbate 80 and chocolate in my pack reeked.

I was, in this ecosystem, prey. And like all prey, the stragglers are the endangered; the meals. How did I know I was prey? You pretty much can't spend an hour in a restaurant, home, or lobby on the North Slope without hearing the polar bear mantra repeated. It is invariably uttered in the bland tonal register of the Pledge of Allegiance, whereby local and visitor alike will tell you with a shudder and a firearm caliber calculation, "Polar bears are the only bears who will seek out a human as a meal. They are the number-one predator on the ice."

And it's evidently not much of a Free Range. Talk was rife in Barrow that two bears had been shot by whaling crews in the previous few days after skulking around the humans' delicious-smelling camps. The animals are evidently such masterful hunters they can crouch, unseen, inches away, in crags between the chunky pressure ridges that are forced up by colliding frozen plates along the shore of the Arctic Ocean's Beaufort Sea.

So I decided then and there to stay right in the midst of the group for the rest of the ride. I nipped the throttle and catapulted myself forward. When I caught up with the caravan again about three miles from the House of Leavitt, I found myself alongside a teenage boy. He was standing on the runner of the bulky twelve-foot wooden sled affixed to the back of a snowmachine, and steering with his feet to avoid obstacles just as dog mushers do. The boy was cloaked in an oversized parka bearing the evil symbol of the Dallas Cowboys. It was heartbreaking to see any connection to Jerry Jones out here in such a beautiful place, but I tried to remind myself that symbols can mean different things in different paces.

Falling into line behind the sled, it occurred to me that I wasn't aware of arctic following-distance etiquette. All traffic laws in bush Alaska are rough guides, mere suggestions, though there are always intangible codes and local customs whose subtleties I was not yet aware of. But soon enough I recognized that one's hazards on pack ice are not very different from those on the "paved" Alaskan winter road, which had flipped me into no less than four ditches in the previous five months. So I tried to give the boy some space, which was a good thing, as with each elder-popping leap over an ice ridge, his sled would shit a Pepsi can or two out of a bucket inside.

I had to watch my back, too. Some young kids were following on a

Pack Ice Driver's Ed

140-horsepower Rolls Royce of a machine at what could only be called tailgating distance. A stop, or falling off my machine, would mean instant calamity for a lot of people in a multi-snowmachine pileup.

* * * * *

Judging by the ease with which the lead snowmachine wound its way across the ice, the trail to the Leavitt whale camp was a thoroughfare. But it was not marked in any organized fashion that I recognized. It would be dotted now and then, when necessary, with a paint-stirrer tipped in bright color, as the progressively higher, winding hillock monasteries of ice often made the next turn in the trail invisible. But even once we veered sharply north away from the flatter ice and through the smashed-together pressure ridges that announced a nearby lead close to 8:15 A.M., it felt to me like the trail only got less defined. Clearly someone knew the ice like I know the road to Homer. (Leads are the narrow channels of liquid—where the aquatic action is—that form between floes of pack ice in the Beaufort Sea: the Arctic Ocean is essentially "on the rocks.")

We made frequent stops along the route, probably every ten minutes. I remember the light conversation with the Leavitts during these caravan-wide halts, which occurred whenever someone had to tie down some loose article or child that had been blowing around in the wind. The chatter with the folks closest to me got friendlier every time, usually on the topic of whether I was cold.

By our third caravan stop, at maybe a little past 8:20 A.M., I was feeling the familiar contrast of pace that washes over me whenever I'm exposed to well-honed indigenousness. Especially pace of speech. The contrast is pretty simple to explain. Simply immerse a Cheechako—with eighteen years logged in perhaps the noisiest, fastest-talking culture in human history—in a subsistence village, Cajun or Eskimo or anywhere. And watch what happens.

Folks of the indigenous mindset, because of cultural handicaps like few lawyers and only recent exposure to March Madness, tend to give thought to questions asked them by fellow *Homo sapiens* without preconceived outlines of the possible rote answers. This leads to some extra processing time prior to verbal answer. You can't hear mental craning; true listening is silent. In short, indigenous people think the actual question over before replying. The pleasure and confusion I feel when confronted with this pace results in a phenomenon I call Third Question Syndrome.

The way it usually goes is this: I ask a question. Then I wait so long for an answer, I believe the question has gone unheard or for some reason ignored (sometimes up to three full seconds), and I start to nervously ask a second, and perhaps less controversial question. I had already had opportunities, since bursting into Annie's house, to actually inhale in preparation for delivering my third question before the answer to the first one cut me off. The answer is usually delivered lucidly and insightfully, often with a twist I might not have caught had I not been shocked into paying close attention. Hence the name Third Question Syndrome.

A specific example of how Third Question Syndrome goes when all parties are conversing at their conditioned pace can be seen in an exchange I had with Annie while I was waiting for the snowmachine. In the Leavitt kitchen faintly redolent of seal oil and "bagels," I bundled up in my extra layers as she had suggested (it turns out very wisely). When I had snapped the final snap on my turquoise pants, I asked her if she thought I was good to go now. She kept kneading and kneading the bread she was working on. I thought she didn't hear me. Still getting no response almost two seconds later, I nervously moved on to my next few questions, which I hadn't yet formulated. "Er, are you . . . st . . . does your family mind . . . are the whales . . . how long have you lived . . . ?"

"A lot depends," Annie said just then, which felt like some time the following week, "On your circulation. And if you're used to the way the wind blows out there." Which turned out, for me, to be not just a pretty true statement, but a pretty important one.

Pack Ice Driver's Ed

Third Question Syndrome continued to prevail throughout the early part of my initial whaling experience. For instance, every time our snow-machine caravan stopped on the ice, Loyala, or whoever was closest to me, looked over and met my eye. I, of course, was full of questions, like, "Where are we?", "Where are we going?", and "Does anyone have an extra pair of sunglasses?" I found myself locking my teeth in resistance to a part of my brain that was saying, "Talk, don't listen." By keeping my trap shut, I learned where we were, where we were going, and that everyone only had one pair of sunglasses.

I had many more opportunities to face the forced pacing of Third Question Syndrome while we hauled to land (or, in local terms, "put up") what turned out to be the 46.5-foot male bowhead possibly more than 100 years old that the Leavitt crew had hunted. This became foremost on everyone's mind, and my conversational conventions had to give way to the rhythm the rather mammoth task demanded. Listening, I found, is a necessary Step Two trait.

* * * * *

I could tell we were almost at the Leavitt camp by 8:30 because the whole world was turning aqua. The wind was picking up, too. Chunks of pressure ridges were sending whistles of arctic breath off the pack ice right through the intermolecular spaces in the rubberized soles of my year-and-a-half-old, recently sprayed Vasque hiking boots. This was a problem all day. An increasingly serious one.

Two evenings earlier, I had tested the actual air temperature on the North Slope by leaving outside overnight a Frappuccino of JM's that had been tucked in the side pouch of my daypack since Homer: it wasn't frozen in the morning. But the chill was vicious. Annie had been right on target. Circulation, indeed. It was all about the wind exhaling off the granular, Styrofoam-corn-like ice. It marauded in off the ocean, too, as if through twisting vacuum tubes. Conditions had all the Eskimos in

Canadian Sorel boots. For the unprepared, by which I mean me, the blood in the feet began to solidify the moment after stepping off the snowmachine.

Nothing against the Vasques, which were holding up just fine after eighteen months of carrying me from Guatemala to Fritz Creek. Their main structural problem was the too-short replacement laces I had bought just before the trip. They only allowed me to lace up one of my three ankle eyelets, which had some chilling Italian Ice spillover results. And canvas and thin suede over molded soles just weren't the right materials for the situation. Three pairs of socks is the way to go, if you ever find yourself on arctic pack ice in year-and-a-half-old hiking boots.

Snapping me out of my grumbling about deficient footwear as we looped around a three-story pressure ridge was a sudden crystalline navy blue set against the rest of the universe. The Arctic Ocean.

I had this strange feeling that an unused part of my mind was filling up with the sight. This was a body of water I never expected to see. I hadn't even been convinced it was real. I had suspected it might be map filler. Or else full of serpents. Maybe this contributed to the dreamlike feeling of pack ice existence for me. Whatever it was, at this moment as I clutched my snowmachine handlebars for dear life, I felt a surging exhilaration at the sensation of newness, at the feeling that even our little old Earth is a pretty big place.

The ocean lead separated, in its narrow line, the one big cloud of ash gray at the false horizon from the blue-white glow of ice on the ground before it. The visible world was disappearing again as we rumbled the last half mile into the Leavitt camp. This misting over quickly made the ocean look something like the slot in a jailhouse visiting room window. It was about 8:40 A.M. when we arrived at what, by any stretch of reasoning, can only be called the end of the line.

As the caravan slowed along the water's edge, the arctic spring weather was fascinating me. Every six or seven hours since I'd arrived

Pack Ice Driver's Ed

in Barrow the sun would suddenly try to burn through in a defiant but weak salmon circle, then would give up again for a while in the milky stew that is the usual atmosphere of the region. Now, just ten minutes after everything seemed clouded up forever, our star made its vain attempt right as we arrived at whale camp, like a well-intentioned directional beacon that is low on batteries.

Somehow, despite the nearly constant blanket draped over the sun, the cloudy-fog layer magnified the reflective intensity of light and made the now three-toned world extremely difficult to look at directly without glasses. Which I didn't possess. I began to seriously worry about snow-blindness and long-term corneal damage.

Billy's flag was already planted in the tallest mountain of jumbled ice boulders within the frost meadow of the Leavitt camp (which was three football fields or so of coastline). It was chopping in the arctic wind as the caravan ambled toward a cluster of people near the water. The banner featured a navy border around a white X with a red dot. It was made by a Leavitt aunt in attendance at the camp, and as much as anything was indicative of the proper restroom location. I felt I was finally looking at a spot on my home planet that would probably not be lined with condos the next time I visited.

I surveyed the sizable snowmachine and sled parking lot that was materializing beside an aged white canvas tent as I edged in at five miles per hour or so to find a spot. I hoped I didn't have to parallel park. I couldn't help but notice with pride that based on the forearm-length nylon sleeves attached to my handlebars, mine was the only snowmachine equipped with the hand warmer option. I hadn't had the chance to fiddle with this feature on the ride in, but now I thought, "What a cool perk, in the event it gets even colder and more windy later on." Which switch had the rental agent pointed to for that? Oh well. One thing I knew was that I didn't have time to worry about it now. There were, you might say, bigger things to think about.

Chapter 6
Food for Thought

With a vague sense of unease I hit the kill switch on my snowmachine. As soon as I looked up, like a smack to my sense of proportion, there it was. The object of our journey, a floating Step Two metaphor made physical. The whale lay like a massive black lump of soap in the water forty feet west of the one structure on the ice—the white tent. People were clustering around it and talking in quiet voices, the way serious car lovers might analyze the finer points of a '57 Chevy at an auto show.

Even with displacement lessons in the bathtub as a kid, I couldn't formulate an exact sense of how large it was, but it was beyond bulky. Bowhead, researchers say, get up to sixty feet, and an adult of more than forty feet weighs a ton a foot. To me, this is an astounding proportion representing flesh of nearly heavy metal density. The biological plan, I guess, is to keep warm in the Arctic Ocean. It is also a figure in which I came to believe over the course of the next eighteen hours of hauling and tugging, slicing and grappling.

For now, I was having a hard time believing I was standing next to an Earth-based animal this big. Factored against everything I'd ever seen on land, it was like something out of a monster movie. This was a creature of such heft, you could start a stroll along its back, list all the concrete accomplishments of the U.S. Congress in the last fifteen years, and still be moving. I tried this, later in the day. This whale was an animal who'd had space to grow.

For ten minutes I listened to the Leavitt crew of four recounting the story of the kill. I heard that our whale was 46.5 feet long, which meant a 93,000-pound meal. Step Two, indeed. As the crew Free Ranged, a more conventionally sized gull gracefully fought the wind above us. Comparatively, it looked like a hummingbird. Or maybe a bee.

During this time, the "bow" of the bowhead was poking out of the surface of a perfectly clear tidal lagoon like a chubby back-floater near the ice. The first thing anyone said to me at whale camp as I stood around feeling superfluous came from an exuberant, constantly chuckling in-law named Emma, who greeted me beside the whale with, "You made it. Now you've got to put that whale up."

"Alone?" I asked, a little afraid. At this point in blown-away visitor mode, I would've politely done anything anyone had asked me to do at the whale camp.

Emma laughed to let me know she was in fact just messing around. I remember her for this endearing chuckle. Then she picked up the radio mouthpiece while everyone assembled (and I lay a quarter-pound Cadbury bar on a sled like an offering). She screamed, "Yahoo! (pause to laugh) Praise God and Hey Hey! We're ready to go here at Leavitt camp! *Aarigaa!*" Just in case anyone in Barrow didn't know. I saw that Chuckling Emma was the psychic Roseanne of the clan: a very strong female presence.

Her announcement got everyone pumped, and I didn't even have time to ask any embarrassingly naive questions about Step Two or anything like that. We just started putting up the whale right then and there at 9:00 A.M. sharp. Or, stated differently, with the help of a small skin boat attached to an outboard motor tillered by a wind-deafened man (he couldn't hear the directions everyone was yelling to him), we proceeded to demonstrate several of the many ways that twenty-nine people cannot manually lift 93,000 pounds of submerged dead whale onto pack ice.

A single pulley didn't work. Nor did a 140-horsepower snowmachine tied to the mammal with a rope. Not even a Cheechako *Tunnic* swimming under the whale and pushing would do the trick, which was a technique suggested by a cousin named Max and vouched for as effective by several experienced men.

Over the course of the morning, we sliced fist-sized holes in the fluke, tied ropes through them, formed a huge tug-of-war line and heaved at

46.5 tons of dead fat. That's a workout. I did the math: 29 people, each able to bench-press, let's be generous, 200 pounds, comes to 5,800 pounds, or about three tons. We were 465 people short. I also hadn't seen, in any of my visits to Ulmer's Hardware, 93,000-pound test rope. Yes, tracking, killing, tying, and transporting a 46-foot whale was no sweat. The tricky issue was apparently hoisting it out of the Arctic Ocean. I began to see why Annie was so willing to have me along.

∗ ∗ ∗ ∗ ∗

To my inexperienced eyes, the group of humanity appeared stumped for a couple of hours. The whale wouldn't budge. I saw later that the whale was being slightly repositioned so that the apparatus that did move it could be attached to it. (The apparatus in question was a giant sling attached to your basic four pulley block-and-tackle system. Whale-butchering is all about leverage.)

The head-scratching discussions about how to do this gave me further opportunity to get to know the people around me. I already knew I liked the Leavitts, from the chats we'd had over eighteen windswept miles. But when Marylou, the young woman who had earlier invited me to ride with the infirm in the sled, yelled, "Free Willie!" after a fruitless heave at the whale carcass, I realized I had come 7,000 miles from my place of birth to hang out with people who were very much like me.

There was the instant familiarity, bathroom talk, seafood addiction, considerable goofing off, relentless jokes of mixed quality, and several of the other characteristics that would be found in my tribe if its original genetic source were ever identified. Although few of the Eskimos felt that the May morning called for full Zapatista facial masks.

It was my first time whaling (all the classes had been full in high school), and I learned what was really going on, organizationally, from several of the women in the family. Different Leavitt females had different methods of shooting the breeze with a shaggy *Tunnic*. With Marylou, it was practical joking: she started right off telling me the wrong things to do, and stopped me just before I embarrassed myself. For example, at about 10:15 A.M. she briefly had me tugging a towline that wasn't tied to the whale, or to anything at all. It's possible I was being tested. Not so much about whether I was competent at whale butchering, but about whether I could take a joke.

Oliver's cousin Margaret was the historian of the group. I forged a strong connection with this gentle human. She was a small, middle-aged, crisply intelligent woman, who just appeared next to me around 11:30 A.M. There on the line, or anywhere in camp, she kept giving me the most interesting background on what I was experiencing.

I want to say that Margaret opened up because I obviously liked her fresh boiled *muktuk* (I find appreciating cuisine is a common form of cross-cultural bonding, along with playing the Allman Brothers and helping with the dishes). But I got the sense she started trusting me well before we reached the eating stage. Maybe it was because she sensed my interest was genuine. Or maybe she was just friendly.

From Margaret, I learned that Captain Oliver was, for the second year in a row on the day his crew landed a whale, eighty-five miles away from his boat. In fact, he was at his hunting cabin for a long weekend in the pristine wildlife-soaked wilderness that the misguided individuals who think they run the United States' resources call the National Petroleum Reserve and opened for oil drilling in 1998. Oliver was starting to recognize a pattern, she intimated, and took his little vacations to ensure the crew would strike. That's how he whales: when he goes away, very far away from the Arctic Ocean, Billy strikes a bowhead with a harpoon. They've got it down to a science.

Margaret had the softest voice I had ever heard. I had to lean forward to catch not just what she was saying, but that she was saying anything. In her diminutive stature, flower-patterned dress, and meek demeanor, she didn't appear at first glance like the wealth of information she was. But after a couple of hours, I learned to grab my notebook any time I saw her approaching, rope or dripping ulu blade in hand, pursed half-smile on her lips, wiping whale oil on her dress. A teacher by trade, she sketched around a story's essence like a silhouette portrait artist, leaving me to pull out the center. Especially when personalities or feelings were involved.

Through the day Monday and into Tuesday, Margaret continued volunteering information in our ad hoc discussions. She almost shrugged whenever she revealed something fascinating to me like, "Everyone around you here is a descendant of two brothers from the commercial whaling days, named Tukak and Inugarak." That helped explain the inside jokes and the absolute informal relaxation down to body functions I found so familiar. It also explained the occasional under-the-breath muttering, usually around instructions over block-and-tackle adjustments. In addition to the propagation of culture and the essential harvest of the primary food source, this was also the family picnic. I was amazed there wasn't more violence.

Margaret and Marylou were only two of the Leavitts who were so friendly to me. From the teenage and twenty-something girls, a few of them already moms, I learned the requisite bad words in Iñupiaq. This mostly occurred in the cozy futon-lined tent, in which a huge pot of duck soup was simmering through the morning. I knew several ways to indicate fornication in Iñupiaq before I could say "good-bye." A page in my notebook is lined with unprintable bilingual words and phrases. I remember really liking Iñupiaq-accented English: the hard final consonants were soothing to me, in a phrase like "ForgeT abouT iT."

I came to love the tent where we gathered at breaks to warm up. Everybody did. It was so snuggly against the biting wind outside, and so quiet beyond the hiss of the stove gas, I could imagine that conception in such a place, amidst mounds of fur and blankets, was not a rare occurrence.

Food for Thought

I took my third tent/thaw break by midmorning. The whale had barely budged, but I wasn't discouraged. This trip was already worth it, I thought, even if the airline ticket cost a month's column-writing. Even if we couldn't put up this particular whale. I was still learning a lot about Step Two. Just from watching Emma season the duck stew.

* * * * *

And then, just when I was wondering if all this tugging was being secretly filmed as a practical joke on the Cheechako, it started to work. Twenty-nine of us began to actually have an effect on the whale mass. This happened around 11:30, after a morning with very little progress. The block-and-tackle system was the ticket, spreading the weight around so we could gain a few inches at a time. The Godzilla-sized canvas sling was looped under the whale's belly. Our tugging rope extended from this.

The system may have been effective, but it was slow going. No one cheered when the fluke and tail were clearly elevated onto the ice close to 1:00 PM. There was so much more to go. We shot each other grim looks of satisfaction. Heaving and readjusting a lot of blocks and knots was in our future. One by one.

It didn't take very long to realize I was amidst the peak of human achievement in the realm on Knowing How To Do Things. Cleverness of the technical variety was being displayed with split-second timing on the ice at a rate of about once every ten minutes the whole day and night of May 17 and 18. I found myself paying very close attention to everything that was happening on this Cheechako field trip. And, with mixed results, I tried to help.

Just before noon, for example, a four-foot hole-boring gasoline-powered corkscrew auger, which would allow the construction of a small ice tunnel to anchor our tugging rope on the shore, needed to be sharpened and thus taken apart, despite the lack of the proper Allen wrench. As we crouched over the machine and deliberated our options, I smelled the watermelon bubble gum many people around me were chewing. Someone handed me a piece. I felt oddly initiated and renewed my concentration. Perhaps I had passed Marylou's test after all.

I watched as the hivelike group effort came down to one individual—and there seemed always to be exactly one—who could solve whatever problem would have dismantled the whole operation and left the season's omega-3 fatty acids decaying in the shallow tidal lagoon at the edge of the lead.

In the case of the giant corkscrew sharpening project, my grand effort to fetch the incompatible Allen wrench I had in my daypack (for my bicycle seat) ended in an unimpressive moon walk slip-slide into the small hole the corkscrew had begun to bore before its dullness revealed itself. While Loyala helped me up, Hubert, I think it was, an actual nonvacationing member of the Leavitt crew, whipped out a screwdriver of just the right size from some secret pocket and pried the machine apart. This was one of the great things about group indigenousness: my failure would only have mattered if no one had succeeded. Instead, my slip was forgotten, except for mouths forming into little Os every time I passed by folks for the next couple of hours.

Hive activity returned as the corkscrew pieces spread over the ice and blade sharpening commenced. I rubbed my thigh, sore from both sword and my fancy-schmancy newfangled hotel key card in my trousers pocket somewhere under the plastic pants Annie had made me put on.

Once the corkscrew had done its task and we had set up the block-and-tackle system before noon, the heave-ho action took on a circular motion. Each person, upon reaching the end of the towline, dropped the rope and jogged back to the free spot closest the whale to resume tugging. It was remarkably effortless for the first few rotations around the line when everyone was in sync. When it became decidedly effort-ful as we exhausted the pulley slack, it was again time for readjustment and coffee, in anticipation of another few inches of progress. This is how we spent the afternoon of May 17.

* * * * *

It was a noncorporate and, I think, very healthy work ethic at whale camp. I'd define the operation as breaks punctuated by intense bursts of energetic full-mind, full-body work. It was also necessary to do it this way, it seemed to me: a whale harvest requires physical concentration and multilevel decision-making that is hard to sustain over time.

Heaving and other tasks were conducted in amorphous shifts of unspoken duration. When you felt like sitting out for a breather, you did. In a group situation, there was room for this self-determined work schedule, and organizing could be left to a rotating council of a few people at a time. Every half hour the whole camp seemed to tire of yanking at blubber, and everybody waded back to the snowmachine yard or to the tent for a ten-minute snooze.

When the mass break felt like it was over, we—men and women, old and young—would walk back wordlessly and play tug-of-war with the whale again. It was strenuous, but I never felt overworked during the entire day. We all knew it would get onto the ice somehow. Englupiaq encouragements amounting to, "KeeP iT uP!" and "Don'T stoP yeT!" would pierce the air and immediately catch the wind when the going got tough.

* * * * *

As the putting up progressed, I noticed I wasn't only absorbing Step Two cues. I also found myself watching closely how humanity's most ice-friendly denizens handled the ice. It seemed a prime opportunity for a demonstration of safe arctic behavior—a subject on which I could use massive consulting. To my surprise, the Leavitts' noses ran, and they wiped them, usually with tissues. And a number of Leavitts even slipped on the ice.

"Brother," I cried in shocked appreciation, embracing an elder who'd cracked through up to his thigh in a thin ice incident around 2:00 P.M., when we had maybe one-fifth of the whale put up. One gets into a particular mindset when realizing that even on "solid ground," one is basically at sea. Barely perceptibly, we were all floating away. Animal, plant, land. It's true everywhere on a drifting planet, I suppose. But I had never before been in an ecosystem where this was so continuously clear. An entire whaling crew learned this forcefully in 1996 when its ice camp became a ship and carried its members out into the Arctic Ocean for some contemplative hours.

There is no way to avoid such mishaps up here, just as there is no way to avoid any element of life, simply because one is 6,800 miles from where people are still a little worried about what their intern might say. Take the human spirit's irrepressible need to kid around.

Playful is the adjective I would use to categorize the Leavitt family attitude. The importance of the task at hand only seemed to increase the jocularity at whale camp. There was almost no subject inappropriate to joke about among these twenty-eight people, and there seemed always time for one more. No one seemed to rush for anything work-related during a joke or prank, except a few times when lines came loose and all our tons of hauling were in danger of sliding frictionlessly back into the water with a scatological *floop*.

My firmest memories from the putting up, in fact, surround the laughter. I'm not sure how essential this is for the successful execution of Step Two, but I couldn't help but take note of it. You didn't know anyone was listening to a particular conversation, but twelve people would all suddenly erupt into a smooth chuckle while continuing to tug at a giant mammal. I really noticed this during my chicken-and-egg conversation with Marylou at about 2:40 P.M.

When she was shuffling next to me in the towline at one, she elbowed me on purpose, so I asked her if she wanted to hear a joke. I resisted the

Food for Thought

urge to ask a second or third question until she eventually said, "Yeah," like three seconds later. I laid on her my newest chicken-and-egg joke, mainly because it's short. It went over well: she belly laughed for about seven seconds and nearly fell down. But then she recovered and confessed sweetly, "I don't really get it."

It seemed that some of the Leavitts didn't have the "Which came first, the chicken or the egg?" mind teaser in their personal lore. Possibly because of the absence of chickens on the pack ice. So all day Marylou forced me to tell the joke to people, and sometimes I had to start it with a preface that delved into the ontological reasons why there even is such a saying.

"You know, it has to do with the unanswerable question of origins: you might throw up your hands exasperated, wondering if the guy started a life of crime because his business fell apart, or if his business fell apart because of his dishonest ways. So, you ask hopelessly, which came first, the chicken or the egg? The first chicken or the first egg? Know what I mean? Was there a chicken first? If so, how did it hatch? An egg? Who laid it?" I might have saved some effort by telling it as "the white-fronted goose and the egg." Plenty of those around these parts.

The joke, which was sent to me via e-mail by my friend Emmanuelle, is this: The chicken and the egg are laying in bed. The chicken, heavy-lidded and looking satisfied, is smoking a cigarette. The egg, frustrated, throws off the covers and storms out of the room, mumbling, "Well, I guess that answers that question."

Well, the joke worked its way down the towline to Billy's girlfriend Loyala at about the time we had the whale's body halfway onto the ice and could see where Billy's harpoon had entered the starboard rostrum. After she processed the punch line, she grabbed the conquering hunter's arm and dragged him over before cajoling me to tell it yet again.

I stayed out of that one.

* * * * *

In this pleasant manner passed the first twelve hours of putting up. It felt like some kind of slow-motion minuet as we circled and circled the ice. Slowly but surely, the entire whale crept up onto the ice. Then, I don't know how it happened, exactly. But suddenly, at around 9:00 P.M., after a short celebratory snack of boiled fluke *muktuk,* I found myself hanging from a grappling hook sunk into the back of a bowhead whale.

I did this while Hubert and others stood on top of the whale eight feet above me and carved *muktuk* into thin, towering slices with an ulu. We rappellers, three or four of us that first time, slowly pulled back the massive strip, still steaming, as each tendon and fatty knot was released. The strip looked like a giant ironing board. It occurred to me that prior to this I had never butchered a chicken.

"Hello, Step Two," I thought. "Nice to meet you."

For a while during the 9:00 P.M. hour, all I could hear from my perch was the *schlushing* sound of ulu working through blubber and the *scrunching* sound of Sorels moving around on ice. It's amazing how quiet twenty-nine people can be. It wasn't brain surgery, on my end of things ("Only brain surgery is brain surgery," Roger had said at one point during Chainsaw Initiation Day), but there was an art to the work some of the Leavitts above me were doing with their ulus-on-a-pole.

In fact, it emerged during the butchering that there were a few fellows who really knew how to carve up a whale. When their hoods were off, they looked in their fifties, with gray shocks of hair and lined eyes. They— Hubert and a man named Johnson especially—were in charge, and when they'd hint at an order from their office atop the whale—in a sort of measured Englupiaq—a ripple of obeisance would issue across the camp.

These guys were skilled butchers on an almost ridiculously large scale. I watched the fox-collared Hubert hold a nephew from making a certain vertical cut by indicating with a raised eyebrow and a pointed finger that the proper slice was through a line of fluke-side tendon.

Food for Thought

"That'll be a nice T-bone," Hubert observed with a Homer Simpson drool when the correct tendon was severed.

"Breakfast tomorrow?" I suggested to him from below while clinging to an eye-endangering grappling hook, waving my free hand to indicate the whole whale.

"Lunch, too," he replied with a twinkle in his eye.

I tended to agree. *"Aarigaa,"* I said, awkwardly checking my notebook for pronunciation as I dangled. Hubert, looking down, grinned.

We were just so glad to have the thing put up, defying what seemed like most of the laws of inertia in the process. Not that we had taken much of a break to relish the moment when the whale was totally on the ice, which had surprised me. I thought we had earned a sort of intermission snooze, or perhaps a gala ball. Instead, the instant the head had reached ice, Emma called, "Hey hey hey hey!" into the radio. Within ten minutes of this heartfelt observation, the processing of the meat began. The thinking seemed to be, "The sooner we start this marathon, the better chance we have of finishing before next whaling season."

When my first strip of *muktuk* released after a twenty-minute struggle, I stepped back from the whale, my grappling hook dripping flesh, and watched from a momentarily wide-angle perspective the doggedly mellow activity at the Leavitt whale camp. These people, who almost never said, "Um, Val-U-Meal Number Two, please," looked pretty healthy to me. Hmm. Tough to figure out why. Very little Polysorbate 80 in this diet. At this time of year, at least.

As I was thinking this, I said, "I don't mind if I do" as a twelve-year-old named Crystal offered me another square of the dense, oily *muktuk* she kept bringing around the camp on a steaming hors d'oeuvres tray. I drew my sword and speared a piece. The high-powered lipid cubes were carved and boiled up fresh by Emma and Margaret in the tent. Even though aquatic mammal was completely unfamiliar to my system, the treat felt nice in my belly and immediately sated me, for about three days.

To a devoted seafood fiend, the two-toned *muktuk* tasted like the smoothest sushi imaginable.

Munching off my sword-ke-bab and dripping whale oil, I examined the fully landed animal carefully, circling it. We had the relationships mixed up, it seemed to me for a second. This whale should be eating us. And Margaret at this moment shuffled up to tell me that before block-and-tackle systems, the whales had been carved up *in the water*.

The beached bowhead looked to me like a smirking mischievous man that Gary Larson might draw, with its baleen rack like a bucked lower fang, which to some degree it is. Just trying to take the fellow in, I couldn't conceive of how the rostrum and extended maxillary bone and 600 baleen all came together. It was the result of extremely deep differential equations. A truly beautiful animal.

This spurred three thoughts almost simultaneously as I gaped at our exercise in disproportion. The first was that, in Step Two, we were talking about one sentient mammal killing another. An obvious conclusion, perhaps, but I most acutely felt it when I started to see and smell the inside of the animal. I had to accept that or go back to shrink-wrapped supermarket whale meat. Another crucial Step Two lesson, Roger Longhenry told me later.

I didn't want to fight this sadness inside me, so I just thanked the whale, and hoped that its family and pod were okay. Five minutes later Crystal pointed to the lead and I saw a new whale pod arcing and sur-facing past us. I remembered that a few days earlier another Barrow whale captain had told me that he talks to the pod as he hunts. He said he asks if he can have one of them to feed a lot of people. And the answer he told me he gets with each breach is, "It's okay. One whale is sustainable." It made me feel better.

My second thought during this rest was that the putting up had just been the relatively easy first stage. Now we had to get the forty-six tons into bite-sized, or at least boulder-sized packages. We were clearly into an all-night activity, at least. Which isn't too bad, when you consider that it's meat for four months, for everybody.

But the real work was just beginning, I realized with perhaps slightly more enthusiasm than the people who had known what we were in for all along. Our chessboard of a *muktuk* snack, which had bloated twenty-nine people to bursting, hadn't even put a dent in the carcass; we had eaten maybe 1/100 of 1 percent of the bowhead. Talk about leftovers.

The third thing I became aware of at this time is that I had been working on a frozen world in thin hiking boots for thirteen hours now. My feet had been borderline frozen for twelve of them. I tapped my toes into the ice to see if I could get any nerve response at all. I might have felt something, in my right pinky. As a new rain of whale innards began to settle over me, I thought back on something a college roommate had once said, lying amidst the detritus of a dorm party, when told he was at that moment missing a midterm exam: "There is, I suppose, a price to pay for being this happy." Or in this case, this Step Two savvy.

* * * * *

Rising mountains of muktuk and meat were forming to Jolly Green Giant proportions by 11:00 P.M. A four-foot sectioned strip of maroon meat surrounding what looked like the liver was at the moment requiring myself and five others to drag it semi-successfully fifteen yards to the appropriate pile. It was comical, like watching mimes pretending to be hauling something heavy, to see a half dozen full-grown men sweating and struggling as they dragged a small cube of red meat a short distance across relatively frictionless ice to a three-foot high mound of the same meat that was *one guy's share.* Or so Chuckling Emma found it.

At this point I really came to believe in the nearly nuclear-rod density of the meat. Life on the North Slope was indeed making me feel a little better about the prospect of harvesting a mere half-ton moose bull back on the Kenai Peninsula come fall, or the following fall, or whenever I was first to be successful at a Step Two task.

It wasn't as funny from my side of the hook, though. You had to be quick as a harvester, both on the whale's back and on the ground: as a piece of meat released, it would often turn, so you had to find and rip out your entrapped hook from the flesh, and reposition it for the next lug. That is, if you didn't want to twist your arm like a rubber band propeller, or have five hundred pounds of blubber land on your knee. Compromising my focus was the fact that I was trying to pay attention to the angle of Hubert and Johnson's cuts, in case the animals in my neck of the woods had roughly an analogous topography.

Not a lot of talking was going on during these first few hours of carving and portion-dividing. Sometime pushing 1:00 A.M. Tuesday, I found myself dragging a uranium-heavy piece of flank with Max and Billy. Actually we were sort of push-kicking it like prisoners attached to a ball and chain. I kept having to stick my hands inside the barrel-sized cube in order to reposition my hook, which was slicing through a piece of blubber.

"This is the last day for these gloves," I analyzed, although that gave me until August 2, technically. I tried to wipe them off on my Space Age pants. Then I looked over at Billy and smiled. But Billy's smile faded after a second. It was something about the blueness in my lips, I'm almost sure of it.

"How're you holding up, toes-wise?" he asked with a slightly worried version of the smile now restored to his face. He had been breaking the ice with me, so to speak, all day, by observing that my boots didn't look very warm and that I should try the locally favored Sorel boots. This was the first time I realized he wasn't just kidding around.

I wanted to tell the truth, which was, "Much colder, thanks. Colder by the minute, in fact."

Instead I only said, "I'm going to wear Sorels next time."

He nodded.

Food for Thought

Billy was half the age of crew members Johnson and Hubert and had the something to prove of the coach's son. He was already a reputedly highly skilled hunter and was particularly proud of this year's hefty kill. Margaret whispered that he had felt bad that last year's kill was to his mind too young a whale. In his interactions with me, Billy just struck me as a fun fellow to hang out with.

"What's a little hypothermia among friends?" he asked me as our hooks began to elevate us up the side of the whale.

"It's a happy hypothermia," I agreed.

The thing was, I was also getting a little worried that it was a real hypothermia. It was close to 1:45 A.M. when I started dangerously shivering, because my feet had been soaked and then supercooled so many times, and then abused more than dried by the arctic wind. My socks were frosty whale platelet Sno-cones. They had formed pressure ridges of their own.

Furthermore, the frost had by now crept up from my feet to chill most of my body. By this point I couldn't write much from my agreeable snowmachine-seat desk on my breaks: my fingers went numb at the distal phalanx within one of my gee-whiz sentences about what a piece of cake organ transplants could be, if every medical student studied bowhead anatomy. When I walked, I could hear my spongy feet slapping like Gollum with each step.

"Nothing to do but keep harvesting," I said to myself. As always, I was willing to die in order to stave off impressions of Cheechakoness.

But I wasn't fooling anyone. "Only thirty-two more feet to go," Max said to me encouragingly, slapping my Space Age–fibered back with a bloody hand and then adding more quietly after he has passed, "Only thirty-two tons. No sweaT."

I and the others peeled backward as the men above us sawed expertly away on the outdoor chopping block. A chunk of blubber released and sploshed wetly against my chest before landing below my feet. My electric blue parka, face, pants, hair, and boots were now covered in whale blood, fat, and guts, great sticky gobs of which I soon transferred to my notebook, which contained Step Two notations that I couldn't decipher when I got home.

* * * * *

By around 2:15 A.M. on Tuesday, May 18, I was trembling in a continuous full-body convulsion. I slightly pulled a stomach muscle from it. I thus hopped down from the whale and took stock. I had no choice but to listen to this message my body was rather urgently sending me, and I started a cycle of ducking every ten minutes into the white tent.

When I emerged slightly defrosted from the first of these sessions, the world was pinker with muktuk runoff than it had been fifteen minutes earlier, and I blinked in the reflected 2:30 A.M. light. The stacked meat and stained ice, the whole 'scape in fact, was almost brick red; the color suffused even in the transparent ice crystals that drifted lazily in the air on the stinging breeze.

While I was readying my hook again, Marylou skipped by me, whacked me on the shoulder, and said, "Hi. I'm sorry but this is tag and you're 'It.'"

I realized in hearing my scratchy, "No, I'm 'Doug,'" response that I hadn't spoken much in hours. Without noticing when the change came, I was employing a different musculature of consciousness. Normally, at any given moment that you might stop me as I go through life, my conceptual self is likely to be poinging on an electrified, tremulous pogo stick, circling the conversation, looking for added meaning, scanning the horizon, and thinking about when my car insurance payment is due, all while wondering why people don't make more noise about roadblocks to third political parties and if the Knicks are really for real this playoffs. In short, my spirit is highly magnetized, and generally in need of grounding in the most electric sense.

Food for Thought

After nineteen straight hours of Step Two, by contrast, I felt I could sense the movement of the ice shelves under my feet. To do just this, I faced the lead and began a staring contest with a seal in the lagoon. My own indigenousness, it seemed to me, flows in and out like the tide. At some point at whale camp, I had stopped fighting the messages recommending I allow the tide in. There's not much I can hope to do, based on my few unplanned glimpses, to predict when I'll be ready to Listen. All I can say is that for a brief time now and then, I Hear.

My guess is that environment has something to do with it. I was at this point only formulating my second question by the time people responded to my first one. The longer I've stayed in Alaska, the slower my pace has become, and the sharper and truer my thoughts.

I stood in that lagoonside spot so long that I was able to tag a napping Marylou before returning to work.

* * * * *

The horizon had closed in so tight I thought that the mist was trying to hug me, and the world moved down a notch. Even the ocean sighed as 2:40 A.M. rolled placidly around. Someone behind me laughed at a private joke, then a gull called, then the species sounds all mixed indistinguishably in a kind of organic white noise. Three bloody men beside the whale deliberated over a 750-pound sirloin that was proving too much for them to tug. Billy and I slid down from the whale like caped crusaders to help them.

I kept this up through maybe another ton and a half of meat. By the time I felt I had to get back to Barrow a little after 2:55 A.M., the whale looked like it had been sliced through with a wire cutter somewhere around its belly button. By this hour Chuckling Emma had faked some distant relations into coming to help by broadcasting over the radio that we were "almost done, just mopping up." We were maybe 30 percent done.

I noticed a lot of Leavitts paying attention to Emma's announcement.

Few wished out loud that the dern go-getters hadn't landed such a gargantuan individual, but it had been a long day. Even Marylou "Free Willie" Leavitt, a woman with a cell biology whose mitochondria are deserving of further study as a possible future energy source, was losing her voice. This I knew because she screamed, "My vocals are going dead! Don't we have enough meaT yeT?"

I knew where she was coming from. We were indeed bloated with plenty. There was just so much food. I still feel, as I write, this concept of abundance and its meaning.

Like everyone else at the Leavitt camp, I was about a day without sleep now. But my shivering was keeping me on my toes as effectively as a caffeine IV. I didn't know if this should relieve or worry me.

My flight back to Homer was at 10:00 A.M., weather permitting. I knew from experience that the surest way to ensure a sudden clearing was to assume the flight would be delayed. The veiled sun looked about ready to begin its arc back up for the regeneration of the three-month day. It was either leave now or miss my plane, which actually didn't sound so bad. I loved where I was, and apart from my body's lame duck vote, no part of me was asking for a change. There was always the tent in which to defrost. But Marylou was driving back home with a load of *muktuk* and liver and it seemed prudent to join. It was the first caravan to leave the camp in more than twelve hours.

Both because of the human inability to pay attention when following someone else, and because I had been effectively blind during the ride to camp nineteen hours earlier, I wasn't at all confident in my knowledge of the route. In fact, actually getting back to Barrow, exhausted, on a terrain of unstable pack ice during my first trip to the place would be a decided challenge. I figured I'd follow the sight of Marylou's machine and sled and, if wind-blinded again, the sound of her laughter. This decided, I made my way to my snowmachine where it was parked past the tent, and this was noticed.

Food for Thought

"You're not leaving, are you?" Loyala asked, possibly thinking there might be a Leavitt on the planet to whom I hadn't told the chicken-and-egg joke.

"I have to if I can get my snowmachine started," I answered, conveying reluctance as I tied my daypack to the machine with close to the world supply of bungee cords. For some reason I considered my pack falling off onto or into the shifting pack ice the most Cheechakoey thing that could happen.

"Well, I guess that answers that question," Loyala said, still on the chicken-and-egg theme as she skipped off. "Don't forget to send us your photos."

When I was satisfied my pack would survive an Arctic Ocean plunge that I would not, I prepared to fire my snowmachine up. I tried to wipe some whale oil off my fingers on the ice. I made sure not to open the choke. Then I pulled the cord to start the machine just as instructed by the rental agent.

And it (the cord) came out with my arm.

"*Huck*," it said.

That was a sound I had hoped never to hear again, I realized, at about the same moment that I noticed I was holding, quite literally, my life in my hands.

Starting with Annie's openness and the UIC executive's brother's nick-of-time arrival, this trip had possessed a subtle rhythm that was so ideal for learning Step Two that I had periodically thought, "There are five billion people out there who might want some of this karma I've been enjoying up here at the top of the world."

As I stood there on the ice like a statue commemorating Cheechakohood, I found myself thinking that when timing goes this right in this life, it is not to be taken lightly. Well, almost everything should be taken lightly, if possible. But here words just get in the way. Thus I just shrugged and smiled at the cord. Missed planes, frozen feet,

149

hypothermia. It was all part of the lesson. And nothing could take away what I felt I had learned on the pack ice. It went far beyond the mechanics of Step Two. It was a reintroduction to a deep-breathing part of myself that I had misplaced.

Brimming with almost dharmic patience, I strolled over to a coffee break cluster on the ice beside the entrance flap to the tent.

"Er, can I ask you guys something?" I asked a late-arriving teen and his friend, probably a distant relative hoodwinked into attendance by Emma. I held up the dangling starter cord, mimed a pulling motion to indicate mechanical issues, and emitted a fierce *muktuk* burp. The kind Eskimo stared at the marbled ocean and thought about it for a solid three seconds. Then he said, "Sure."

We tromped to my parking spot, be-Vasqued feet slapping alongside well-insulated Sorels, and the kind Eskimo rather confidently set about getting the snowmachine going by stringing the starter cord around a metal wheel somewhere inside the engine, and yawning it out forcefully perhaps forty-eight times.

Huck, went the starter cord.

"Don't open the choke," I advised.

My mechanic studied the machine. His task was to outsmart the guy who had outsmarted the machine's factory starting system by working around the missing key. He had to not just understand the UIC executive's brother's thinking, he had to circumvent it. It was a MacGyver moment.

"Is there some place to prime it?" I suggested ignorantly.

As he worked, the kind Eskimo grumbled about poor engine maintenance, one time so disgusted with what he might have thought was my machine that he stopped to explain to me why (words immediately forgotten) should be connected to (words immediately forgotten) via (words immediately forgotten) for maximum (words immediately forgotten). I nodded scientifically, my oily, now tarry hand on my chin to indicate blue-collar awareness while thinking, "I am so glad people like you exist."

On try forty-nine, the kind Eskimo's friend walked up, opened the choke, and the machine started on the tug. The kind Eskimo dropped the starter cord in my hand as though it were my key being returned at a Manhattan parking garage.

＊ ＊ ＊ ＊ ＊

Marylou was long gone—even out of laughter range. With the mechanical repair and engine diagnostics lecture, I was a solid fifteen minutes behind. I had a decision to make. Get back eighteen miles alone over arctic pack ice, at 3:10 A.M., unsure of the route atop a snow-machine with mechanical problems. Or, what? Spend the night hacking at *muktuk,* in hopes of another caravan leaving sometime before 9:00 A.M. so I could find my way back to Barrow and squish onto my plane?

I needed, I felt, one more big problem. Yes, in this kind of situation, mere freezing, stranding, exhaustion, and directional disorientation aren't enough to spur the clear thinking allowed by total overstimulation of the parasympathetic nervous system.

And I got it, in the form of a news bulletin from Craig George, the chief biologist with the North Slope Borough's Arctic Research Facility, or ARF. Craig, whom I had befriended a couple of days earlier after he had very kindly invited me to ARF's whale census research station, had showed up at the Leavitt camp to collect a sample, as his team does of every whale. An icicles-dripping-off-the-mustache type of Alaskan, this man is never off the clock.

What he told me left me thinking someone else was almost definitely in possession of that karma I had been hogging. Craig had sauntered over to watch the hotwiring machine spectacle. In fact, quite a crowd had gathered to observe the travails of the stranded *Tunnic.* "You know about that polar bear that's been running around this side of Barrow all day?" he asked me, just as I pocketed the returned starter cord.

I didn't. He continued. "You know, we'll be packing it up in the next couple of hours. You can ride back with us."

I thought at first that he was just being friendly. For him, polar bears and whales were as common as chopping wood was for me. I didn't want to put him out. "I dunno, the trail is pretty self-explanatory, isn't it?" I asked.

"Well, yeah, I should say for the most part," Craig answered. "Barrow's that way." He was pointing vaguely southeast.

By now I should've known better than to ask directions this close to Magnetic North. It just left me confused. Nearly all roads lead to the equator from here anyway. But my mind was racing: what if the oft-pondered polar reversal (not to mention the oft-pondered polar bear) hit while I was on the pack ice? I'd travel forever and no one would ever find me. Or I'd be eaten. The way I was seeing it, both sucked.

The engine crackled unsteadily next to me. "Ah, I better head back now," I said. "I have to return my snowmachine before my flight."

Craig's parting remark was a simple, "We'll pick up your remains." Accompanied by a shrug.

"Yeah, you know, that's something I've been meaning to ask," I said. "If I come across a polar bear, can I outrun it on this thing? Do I just gun it, just open her up?" I pointed my arm out straight in front of me three times to indicate extreme speed.

Craig's response was rather more casual than the situation demanded, I felt. "Oh, he won't bother you on the machine. It's when you break down that you're screwed." He peered down distastefully at the disfigured vehicle. He didn't appear to be kidding.

"But I read the Ice Safety Guidelines," I wanted to whine. I looked down at the starter cord protruding from my pocket. He had a point, I was willing to concede. I was holding the machine's second-string

Food for Thought

method for ignition. The traditional implement—a key—was nonexistent.

"And what's your gas level?" Craig asked.

Another, I had to admit, good question. The gauge had been doing that wild "am I empty or am I not?" dance on the ride to the Leavitt camp. And during the kind Eskimo's jump start, churning Iraq's quota of unleaded gasoline for 1999, I thought I had heard him make some editorial comments amidst foreign words like "crank shaft" and "manifold" about the "fuel pump not looking like it's fastened." The kind Eskimo didn't have much use for people who didn't keep their snowmachines maintained.

Still, the decision to leave on my own, though inexplicable, seemed somehow a clear one. I didn't want to leave the whale harvesting job half done (actually about one-third done), but I was getting messages that now was the time to go. For one thing, biologist packing-up time, I had learned on Sunday morning at the whale census camp, operated with a precision that made Homer O'clock look like a Swiss clock. If something scientifically interesting came up (like the chartreuse muck on the whale's baleen, little pieces of which two researchers were at the moment chipping into baggies), the research team would stay as long as necessary to investigate it.

I also felt the growing sense that I had to do something about returning the arguably motorized hunk of scrap metal. I had the feeling it was slightly overdue at the UIC executive brother's. The Ukpeagvik Iñupiat Corporation is possibly the entity you least want to piss off above the 71st parallel.

Plus, there was something appealing about a flat-out run across the ice. As various vehicles had been trying to tell me since Fritz Creek, part of hunting is being able to get to and return from the hunt. In fact, the Step Two "food" component involved an entire umbrella of survival skills I would at some point have to learn.

Not Really
An Alaskan
Mountain Man

So I was going to try to make it back solo. In the name of Mountain Manhood and Relaxed Tone and all of that. I just had to pray that the engine wouldn't die for any reasons I hadn't yet encountered or for any reasons I had yet encountered. It seemed to be at that phase in a machine's life cycle when the whole house of cards could collapse at any minute. I also, I mentally cataloged, needed not to crash, flip, drown, or give in to the urge to make notes until I was snuggled in at the Top of the World Hotel, watching *Biography*. Alaskans who don't have television reception tend to drink it in at hotels.

To slow down was to risk a stall. And I certainly didn't know how to start the thing up by the open-heart-surgery method that the kind Eskimo had executed. Which could be fatal.

I wished with a burning ferocity that I had stuck around at the General Store until some Mountain Person had come along to help Laura with her carburetor pin. How ironic would it be if that part of the engine wound up as my official cause of death? I had to giggle.

"Survive much?" I asked myself, repeating my friend's all-too-apt mantra.

* * * * *

While my snowmachine's engine continued to rip unsteadily, I looked back one more time toward the whale. An unnerving ringing followed each stroke as if a rhythm-challenged percussionist were stuck inside the vehicle.

The softest blue essence emanated as though in convection waves from over the last pressure ridge before the ocean spread and touched the sky. Outlines of Leavitts still carving away atop the whale's back were trimmed by an escaped spotlight of sun and surrounded by snowmachines that were shimmying with mirage consistency. It was a windy quiet, but above my own weak engine I could hear the whispers of ulu blades through blubber at twenty yards. The standing baleen compressed and fluttered in the wind like an accordion dangled loosely from one end, clicking on contraction.

Along the far side of the whale, a multigenerational line of gore-smeared women crouched on the ice, stringing intestines in a line forty yards long before slicing them and packing them in baskets. Closer by, the boy in the Cowboys parka tagged Loyala in an ambush beside the tent and then headed to the pressure ridges. I could make out Chuckling Emma stalking around with a clipboard like a gym coach, jotting the names of other whaling crews that deserved shares of the meat by virtue of having helped tow the Leavitt's bowhead to camp.

Panoramically speaking, all this activity framed one of the more beautiful vistas I had ever seen. It left me feeling pretty good, after first exposure, about Step Two. Ready to give it a go. *Aarigaa.*

Revving the engine gingerly, I briefly dwelled on the social issue of good-byes. I didn't know how to or if I should give them. It didn't seem like bookends had been needed on the hello end. Funny how on the pack ice or in the biggest city, so much seems to be about people's feelings.

How would I say good-bye to three dozen people? Everyone was working and anyway, what would I say? "Thanks for teaching me how to survive?" Maybe so. And all the Leavitts had asked in exchange was that I help tug and grapple a bit.

I wound up feeling that to delineate a stop by saying "good-bye" would only force an artificial break in the activity at the whale camp and exaggerate the importance of my own role in it. So I just wished the Leavitts many a good harvest and streaked off south (soon to be north), mentally noting to include a heartfelt letter with a copy of my photos addressed to Billy's PO box, if I ever found Barrow.

And indeed the trail appeared pretty well-defined under my tracks. There were some maddening forks, but they tended to rejoin one another. That wasn't the problem.

The problem came down to my hands inside my gore-soaked

gloves instantly freezing. I drove for a few minutes, looked down, and though I could swear I saw something bulging at the handlebars, I could feel nothing below the wrists. I was the man with no hands.

As it had on the ice when I tried to make notes with soaked feet and chilled fingers, the blood had moved on and was regrouping at what the mainframe considered more vital organs. It's fascinating but scary to recognize your body doing this. There is no hypothermia override button. You can consciously watch yourself freezing to death.

There was no hand warmer option.

This didn't stop me from idiotically inserting my wet gloves into the phantom mechanism's sleeves. At first I couldn't decide which position on the most likely switch was "on." I tried both positions several times, veering sickeningly as I fiddled with the dashboard at what felt like ninety or ninety-five miles per hour (the speedometer read "zero"). Then I couldn't decide which position of the switch was causing more *cold* air to fly in through the flimsy nylon of the "hand warmer" sleeves, directly onto my hands under sopped black-and-blood gloves.

* * * * *

For a good while, possibly fifteen minutes, I held deliberations, which resulted in the conclusion that the loss of a few fingers was preferable to being eaten by a polar bear. Which meant I couldn't pull over to warm myself up.

"Whoa, bear!" I called from my seat, the way you're supposed to alert what were now seeming the downright gentle brown and black bears of lower Alaska. I was quaking from fear and frost. No, I didn't dare stop.

This decided, I gave myself the shaggy Cheechako version of the classic tough love/Lombardi-style speech: *This is you, right?* I berated myself through frozen lips. *This is what you want to be? How you want to define yourself? This is why you're not a lawyer or a TV critic or some-*

thing? Well, suck it in and do it. You'll either be home in a day writing about it with Sunny at your feet or you'll perish horribly with an expensive return plane ticket in your pocket. Now get out there and NOT DIE!

Sometimes, even with overreacting and pseudo-macho posturing, the situation is serious. The wind-driven frigidity, the numbness, and the building panic were so severe after perhaps another ten post-pep-talk minutes that I could no longer consistently engage the throttle. The dead weight of my frozen accelerator thumb was simply unable to apply force.

Eventually I admitted I had to risk a stop. It no longer had anything to do with bears. In fact, death by mauling would probably be a quick way to go. My life now depended on the neutral gear of a twice-hotwired snowmachine with no windscreen and more in need of a regular tune-up than Dick Clark.

How were labor relations at the Polaris Snowmachine Company in 1974? So much seemed to hinge on this. I just had to hope that a stop wouldn't cause the engine to do anything more drastic than idle. This required a mental focus not unlike what I imagine was required of the first-time paratrooper preparing to take the leap. Around me in every direction were miles and miles of empty blue-white ice. If the engine died, I was simply not capable of restarting it.

"Okay, okay," I shouted through the Marcos mask. "Mechanical knowledge can be indigenous survival knowledge. It's all connected. I'll get on this." I really meant to, in the unlikely event of survival. I made a mental note and dubbed this revelation the Carburetor Pin Lesson. My mind went now to the Jack London situations in which the dogs pick clean the bones of those not adept enough at any one of the Three Steps of survival. I began to get choked up. There is no feeling sorry for yourself like pending-death-through-ignorance feeling sorry for yourself.

I yanked my hand out of the worthless sleeve, let go of the right handlebar that contained the throttle, and started to plane in a decelerating skid. In the end I had to fall back on three things: something I learned from a childhood friend about the armpits being the second warmest part of the body, a comment by Hunter S. Thompson about avoiding sudden starts and stops to maximize fuel economy, and something I recalled from the Knievel boys about body position when hitting air. There were some jumps on the Barrow "trail" that at the speed I was taking them made me feel as though I had just eaten some olestra.

I crunched to a stop. The idling engine, miraculously, continued to chop away accompanied by the distant echoing of its chimelike rattle. I'm no mechanic, but that was no healthy ozone-depleting hum. Jamming my hands under my arms, I distinctly heard a chain jingling around in there somewhere. None of this, I was happy to note, affected the decrepit machine's competition-level zero-to-sixty acceleration.

I emitted a satisfied, masculine scream of agony as blood again began to break through my frozen capillaries. Almost immediately I felt myself able to worry the worries of the merely terrified modern human: Would the front door of the Top of the World Hotel be open this early in the morning? Built with even marginal efficiency, should one B-2 bomber really cost $200 million?

I took a moment to look around myself. The universe, as far as I could see, was as windswept and empty as the end of a European art film. There wasn't even a gull flapping. In terms of no real options, you really can't beat a situation like being stuck alone on top of the world. It was one of those Alaskan landscapes that makes revisiting small states like California and Texas feel like returning to your old room as an adult—the things you thought were large are in fact all very small. I didn't particularly want to dwell on that reality right now.

Sufficiently thawed for the moment, I nicked the throttle and boomeranged myself back toward what I hoped was Barrow. My entire face was numb too, and I had my old problem of inability to see, but these minor inconveniences were manageable. I throttled in ten minute spurts, whose weaves would have served as sufficient proof of DUI in

Food for Thought

any court in America.

The delayed and musical metallic jingle following every hand-defrosting deceleration got worse with each idling: a horrifyingly weak amplitude chop now lurked below the main engine sound, like a pork-eating smoker with extreme arteriolosclerosis trying to breathe. But I kept with the plan. I really had no choice. As soon as I could howl in finger anguish, I knew I was good to go again for another few minutes.

Adding to the ambiance was the extremely low ceiling that had settled in again, giving me, even during armpit pitstops when my eyes dried up, visibility of about eighteen inches. I only drove into one sinkhole as a result of this, and it was shallow enough to allow the machine to temporarily become watercraft (also requiring no license in Alaska) until I emerged on its other side. I landed on the ice a little wetter but still on the machine, thanks to an appropriately left-sloping lean I made while pawing the handle of my sword, ready to use it in accordance with Paragraph Three in the "Ice Conditions" section of the Ice Safety Guidelines. As a seasoned faller, I held awed respect for this simple and practical recommended hole-survival method. I could have used such a technique outside Mako's office back in December.

After the sinkhole escape I braked hard several times like you're supposed to for the squeegee effect after driving an automobile through a deep puddle. For some reason I called to mind at that moment the lamest cliché of ursine safety in the Alaskan backcountry: "You only need to worry about bear attacks if you're the slowest member of your group." The thought was barely out when I swore I heard something rumbling behind me, and I braced myself to imminently discover whether polar bears go for the neck or the viscera. Or else . . .

"This is it," I thought, my mind thumping magnetically and reacting quickly now that I discovered I was still alive. "The poles are switching." I wheeled the snowmachine around, in full belief that Barrow now lay in the opposite direction.

But it had just been my heart pounding—more forcefully than the sickly vibration of the engine. I spun the machine back around and throttled to Warp Factor Three.

* * * * *

When the first wavering form of what looked like it could be a human structure came into view, it was Shangri-La to me. Barrow was *civilization*. I abandoned the machine where it glided to a stop on the icy beach below Number 916. Little tornadoes of trash swirled around me like ceremonial dancers. A solicitation letter from a televangelist blew into my stomach. I sprinted up the Leavitt's hill and waved at the windows of the house in case Annie or Marylou heard the engine.

Anyone paying attention to Barrow's west side at 3:47 A.M. on May 18, 1999, would have seen a male figure, wearing a besnotted Subcomandante Marcos mask, literally stumbling down Okpik Street with a sword on his side, dripping whale oil, and muttering about the recent decline in hand warmer technology. Any of these characteristics of the pedestrian could perhaps in isolation be dismissed as disorientation due to magnetism. But given the complete picture, it's fortunate I am not still in the North Slope Borough drunk tank.

My evening wasn't over. I had to call the UIC answering machine, pretending it was only 9:00 P.M., talk about the great day I had on the brother's excellent machine, and then break it to him that the starter cord was sitting on the dash. I was tempted to ask the executive, given his track record for rounding up equipment on short notice, whether he knew where I could get a good map of the borough at 4:00 A.M. in Barrow. One that showed things from an Iñupiat perspective—looking down, so to speak. Given the pending polar reversal, it might make a nice memento of the Earth when this part of it was north.

It's very rare in this life, I reflected, plopping on the bed and nearly disemboweling myself with my sword, that one gets to make a contact call

Food for Thought

at 4:00 A.M. I felt very nocturnally private eye-ish. Although it was plenty bright outside my window—as usual right when I was about to leave a beautiful place. The mist was lifting to reveal a light blue sky.

What a day it had been. I had been awake for twenty-one and a half hours of it, a distinction which, in retrospect, I wear with honor and oft repeat, but which I don't remember feeling so great about at the time. Maybe that is what rural Alaskan memories principally are: therapy for torture (in this case, what to, say, the Geneva Convention, would be considered clinical torture: sleep deprivation, unsafe work conditions, slave labor, a brutal routine). Indeed, the whole experience bestowed on me a new perspective on pain that morning, which was this: pretty much everything I do in Alaska causes me pain. Physical pain that, in almost any scenario I could've set up for myself in life, I wouldn't welcome into my daily routine. But somehow here, I do. It's part of Alaskan life. The way bad meals are part of air travel.

I had VH-1's *Behind the Music* on when I finished my call. Evidently Led Zeppelin did drugs, and also improvised. The Eskimo Channel announced a raffle whose prizes included wolf and wolverine skins. Toasty under about one thousand geese worth of covers, I was just drifting out of consciousness when CNN started graphically displaying the value of a good map of downtown Belgrade: hundreds of real people were dying in off-target explosions before my eyes, so I switched to the Sci-Fi Channel, on which only imaginary people were dying. I fell asleep wondering how, why, and when the species moved from Step Two concerns to departmental meetings and NATO.

* * * * *

"How did it go?" JM asked, hugging me in the tropical Homer airport back in the lush land of vegetation and premature 1:00 A.M. sunsets.

"Fun," I said, reeking of day-old gore, which I knew was about ten seconds away from making a certain golden retriever mix happy.

"I helped put up a 93,000-pound bowhead whale, and I didn't even miss *Mystery Science Theater 3000*."

"Are you hungry?" she asked.

"I'm stuffed full of whale blubber. Can we eat something light, like a T-bone steak?"

And we did just that after a trip to Safeway, whose fluorescent lights seemed very bright and very yellow, like a school hallway or perhaps the corridor leading to the fifth level of hell. After that we stopped only to rent *Revenge of the Pink Panther*. Then I drove home, turning left where I would normally turn right.

"Just practicing," I explained to JM as we ended up in hubcap-deep mud some ten miles from anything. "For the polar shift." She nodded, seeming to understand.

I settled back in the cabin with its newly thawed and repaired water pipes on the evening of May 18. Like the rest of my world, it smelled like *muktuk* for several weeks. Outside, the moose who managed to survive the first third of 1999 were back, as Sunny was loudly alerting me at 7:00 P.M. They were already fattening up off the deck, some of them pregnant.

In the shower my first morning back in Fritz Creek I smelled *muktuk* scent wafting off me like smoke after a barbecue. Truth be told, I didn't really want to wash the whale smell off me or my clothes: I was in no rush even to clean the blood from under my toenails. I took to making Homer Simpson growls, to the accompaniment of, "Mmmm, fetid whale fat."

Still in the same mind-set, I had guests from Anchorage a few days after my return. I laid out my sleeping bag for them on my bed before being banished to my tent outside. "It may smell a little bit like bowhead," I informed them. "But it's clean." My guests kind of caught each other's eyes. As I wandered in internal exile amidst the spruce that had once swiped my mask and goggles off my head, I reflected, "Most people in the world smell. People are meant to smell."

This new olfactory philosophy thrilled JM when, for example, we were sea kayaking and camping across the bay a week later. Just as the local Ursidae hill denizens were waking up, I was wearing boots whose sea mammal scent we could smell from head height.

"Ah, these are only the gentle brown bears we get down here in the temperate zone," I comforted her. "They're like the Cheechakos of the bear family."

JM stopped on the trail. "What happened to you up there?" she asked me with a laugh. "You're glowing and acting all brave and everything."

"I'm not sure," I replied. "But I think I might've become a hunter." We'd see about that. A shotgun was on my shopping list.

Chapter 7
Nobody Shoot, Nobody Get Hurt

*J*ust when I was revved up to put my Step Two Arctic Field Lesson into practice, I picked up the phone and realized I didn't have Roger Longhenry to consult with anymore. It was two months since his heart condition had become acute and forced him to hightail it to Portland. I only learned on the eve of his departure that he had suffered a heart attack before I even met him. His initial e-mails indicated he had found a satisfactory location midway between the cardiac unit and the Widmer Brewery. He had as yet made no mention of the cathedral job, though he had been positioning himself through careful lifestyle choices closer and closer to it.

With his absence, I felt my Cheechako training wheels removed. I had pictured Roger as my personal hunting advisor, the way Charlie Sheen studied with stockbrokers before the filming of *Wall Street*. Since Chainsawgate, Roger's casual "go for it: everyone was a Cheechako once" attitude had helped spur me to take my first commercial fishing deckhand stint, and to ski down a wilderness peak in some kind of drastically ill-conceived and nearly fatally embarrassing pursuit of Step Two navigational skills. JM and I also camped out with a pack of wolves at 20 below zero one night in Denali National Park.

My new neighbor, Bob, wasn't exactly a Roger substitute. More my contemporary, what I liked best about Bob was his spontaneity. He was willing to drop everything to investigate whatever interested or amused us at the moment. In the three months I'd known him, I didn't think I'd yet heard him say anything but "yes" to any suggestion of adventure, especially if it involved being outside. He never seemed to have trouble getting out of work when I proposed some kind of excursion.

For example, when I told him during a drum session in June that my time with the Leavitts had energized me in the subsistence realm, he raised an eyebrow, Mr. Spock–like, and said, "Premeditated killing. Interesting." Since I had promised the animals of Fritz Creek that my home woods would be a safe haven, Bob agreed to meet Sunny and me in the middle of the Kenai Peninsula wilderness outside the tiny enclave of Cooper Landing. "Just name the day," he'd said.

Bob was a different kind of Mountain Man—specifically, the anarchist, vegetable-growing kind. This would not be the same kind of "blast away" Step Two perspective I would've received from Roger Longhenry. I knew that going in. But what I was really needing for my first foray into gunpowder was a witness. He would be driving north from Homer on the day we agreed to do this. Sunny and I would wind the roughly equal one hundred miles south from midtown Anchorage, where I had just purchased a bulk tower of bathroom tissue and a firearm.

It was the endless daylight of July 1, the world was bursting with wildflowers, and I was gunning for some dietary indigenousness. Like the Leavitts did, I wanted to eat from my immediate environment. That didn't stop me from picking up jerky and other provisions for my hunting trip at one of the chain wholesale warehouses springing up like fungi all over the Frontier. But I wanted this to be the last time I toted Polysorbate 80 for my lunch. I was firm on this point as I wove like a heavily armed Mr. Magoo through Anchorage in the blinding early evening light.

Our hunting pack of two humans and a dog had a destination in mind, though it was vague. The tip came from Odie, proprietress of now-defunct Odie's Sandwiches in Soldotna, a town between Homer and Anchorage on the Kenai Peninsula. Odie's was my favorite food shop in Alaska because of the fresh bread Odie baked while vigorously accompanying contemporary Christian music on the stereo. She had a beautiful voice. I'd stop there whenever I was on my way to Anchorage. In fact, the thought of an Odie's "Turkey-on-Wheat-with-Everything" was often what propelled me off my deck toward town, not normally a high priority for me. But sometimes even a Rugged Individualist needs to stock up on TP.

As she assembled her bowhead-sized loaves, Odie always asked what I was up to and how the travel columns were going. During this particular drive north, I mentioned I was on my way to buy an eating weapon. I also mentioned intentions of becoming a practicing Step Two-ite right after. Odie then told me I might want to explore a remote lake in the heart of the thick forests and wetlands of the Kenai National Wildlife Refuge. It was a spot she and her family favored.

"You won't find anyone there but critters," she said, humming and smiling. "We had to shoot a bear there once that just wouldn't leave us alone. We tried everything. It was very persistent." She made reference to an entrance trail that led to the lake, but had Barrow-like difficulty pinpointing its exact location. I gathered it was roughly in the geographical middle of the Kenai Peninsula somewhere.

My mouth stuffed with one of her magical sandwiches, I started listening intently when I noticed that in describing this place, Odie's face melted into the same beyond-consciousness bliss mine did at the mere thought of the turquoise pond across Kachemak Bay. I was getting psyched, which I knew because the fantasy images were coming fast and furious: myself the Mountain Man standing with be-Vasqued boot atop a trophy bull. Sunny wearing barbecue-sauce-mustache from the moose ribs that sustained her through some long winter.

* * * * *

Only one sliver of trepidation worked its way into my spirit as I left the Anchorage city limits later that day and drove south to harvest flesh: I had yet to hear a glamorous hunting story. "Not even Free Ranged," I reflected as I wound down the Seward Highway past the turnoff for Hope.

This stood hunting braggadocio in stark contrast to, say, your basic fishing tale. Whereas fishing stories generally included fighting a valiant king salmon into the boat, hunting recollections on the Kenai Peninsula usually involved plunging arms into mammals' intestines while trying not to retch. All while in a hurry to get half a ton of meat somewhere before it spoiled and before any nearby bears got a whiff of it.

Typical was a recent story I'd heard from Laura, of course, who filled my propane tank at the General Store while giving an account of the final moments of the paralyzed-but-conscious bull moose her husband had dropped from their deck the previous fall with a shot to the spine.

"He was alive and totally aware," Laura told me in the requisite Relaxed Tone. "The whole time we decided where to deliver the final shot, his eyes followed whoever was speaking. As if we might have a solution to the bewildering situation."

But this was Step Two, I tried to remind myself as I carved the Subaru down the peninsula. Beside me Sunny watched with impressive focus the arctic terns that were banking in inter dimensional formation above us. Here I faced what I had flown practically to the North Pole to come to terms with: the reality that eating another animal pretty much means its death. But had I come to terms with it? Butchering an already dead whale was a lot different from shooting the animal myself.

Eyes. I hadn't considered eyes. There were no eyes looking back at you from an Odie's turkey sandwich.

"No, no," I steeled myself. Laura wasn't going to cow me this time, so to speak. I had my Cheechako mission to consider. The Alaskan Mountain Man hunts his own food. He can sustain himself over a winter with only occasional Odie's sandwiches. He flosses with gristle. That was my view on July 1 at 9:00 P.M. Yes. In short, I was a radical. Like all radicals, I hadn't thought things through. I gave that a shot in the car, as Sunny flew into my lap following a questionable pass of an RV taken at snowmachine bear-evasive speed.

"So I've never really even grown a tomato," I reasoned. "You gotta start somewhere."

Yes, my gun was still in the wrapper, and was made in as scary a factory as anything on the shelves in Costco. Sure, I didn't know exactly how to fire it and was more than a little bit afraid it might backfire or explode when I did and find yet another way to place me on the Cheechako obituary pages. No one ever said there wouldn't be a learning curve. I was willing to accept that, I thought, as I swerved to avoid killing an out-of-season moose the more modern way. And this much really was true: the few times in my life I'd been able to eat locally and organically for a sustained period of time I did feel my healthiest.

* * * * *

I arrived first at our meeting place and started unloading the car, laying the gun against a rock first. I carried it like it was plutonium. My presumptive hunting dog sniffed it curiously and I had to stop her from marking it. The salesman at the gun shop had taken it out of its box as simply as if it had been a pair of trousers, and had assembled it for me as I watched terrified about the reintroduction of the term "kickback" into my life. Then he gave me a firing primer, more of a brief, jargon-packed run-through, in the midst of my flurry of unabashedly liberal questions about the shoulder pain I could expect from recoil. From too much cartoon watching, I envisioned the gun actually knocking me to the ground as soon as I pulled the trigger. God knows where the shot would go.

Bob pulled in a half hour after I did. I was in the shade, and at first he didn't see my clothes, fishing gear, djimbe drum, shotgun shells, Ulmer's ice sword, and firearm scattered around the Subaru, or me pumping my fist at him after the manner of a bowhead tail breach.

I was glad to have safely unloaded the car without incident. On top of my crimped-eared hunting dog sticking her snout out the window, the vehicle had been so full of camping gear, explosives, toilet paper, and killing apparatus when I left Anchorage that it would have justified any law enforcement action in urban or suburban America. I vaguely remembered a time not too long ago when being in possession of a chainsaw surprised me. Now I looked like a Jeep commercial for the *Soldier of Fortune* demographic.

Bob drove almost into the nearby Kenai River, before wheeling around and spotting me. We were lucky to have found each other. He had described our meeting spot only as "the parking lot field there on the Homer side of the river before that turnoff," when I had called him from Anchorage to say I was on my way, and armed.

When he had his truck stabilized and parked, we greeted each other in one of the prettier spots on the planet and Bob made immediate reference to the goal of the excursion.

"Ahhh," he exhaled, after taking in a draught of pristine mountain air. "I love the smell of gunpowder in the evening."

"So you wanna go in until Friday or Saturday?" I asked with relish. I couldn't believe it. I was heading into an expedition, and there was almost no chance of being stranded. We were using our feet, so there were no vehicle maintenance issues. Sunny's presence ensured that we would find our way back to the car, wherever we parked. There were few hassles at all for this project, other than the usual handicap of Homer O'clock.

"Isn't this Friday?" Bob asked.

"I thought it was Thursday."

"Could be. But I thought it was Friday." He stroked his beard, which failed to age him past his twenty-six years. He appeared to be considering the issue intently. "Are you sure?" he inquired.

"Not 100 percent, but I sense from the way people around me have been acting it's roughly late in the week. What day does it feel like to you?"

Not Really An Alaskan
Mountain Man

We both said at the same time, "Saturday." Well, we had one element of rural Alaskan life down. We were hopelessly off Gregorian time.

Bob surveyed my Cheechako-inspired detritus, and then his eye fell on the weapon amongst it, leaning on the mossy rock.

"What do you call that?" Bob asked.

"A shotgun," I explained.

"What kind is it? Is it a *20-aught?*"

I thought in his directness I might detect a hint of sarcasm.

"Twelve gauge," I said. "But nice knowing to use the gun-sounding term 'aught', though."

Bathed in a pleasant 9:30 P.M. light, Bob and I packed up for the hunting trip. I didn't find it strange for a moment that I had selected a mostly vegetarian for my initial hunting buddy. I knew I would be getting honest opinions about the whole process.

"I heard on the radio during the drive up here that animals have culture," he told me, stuffing his sleeping bag. "A department head somewhere has released a study. Shocking, isn't it?"

"Yeah, but now it's official," I said. "Someone with tenure said it."

Bob looked at me as solemnly as if he were about to ask me to be his child's godfather. "It set me thinking. Would you mind if we discussed some of the fallacies of the Adaptionist model of evolution while you blow up some animal culture?" he asked.

"Sure," I replied, cramming my fishing tackle into my old, stained pack.

As always, I was okay with the rural Alaskan quirkiness. I just knew I really wanted a spotter along with me to get medical attention in case I hurt myself or anything else during my hunting debut. I was a sudden and dogmatic believer in the buddy system, because of my gun fear. This was a fear that I noticed was increasing in proportion to my proximity to the actual hunting grounds. The shotgun triggered an immediate, unnatural quiver in my belly when I even looked at it. This

Nobody Shoot, Nobody Get Hurt

complicated the flow of my Step Two juices. I kept seeing the headlines: *Cheechako disemboweled in bizarre backfiring incident. "I don't know how he could have fired it like that," confounded paramedic testifies.*

Also, I suddenly wasn't so sure exactly what I thought about all this potential animal-killing business. I tried to deny it, but Laura's story was getting to me. I was getting the feeling that Step Two was a lot easier when I had twenty-eight lifelong practitioners supervising me on the pack ice.

* * * * *

I couldn't quite bring myself to disclose my wariness out loud. Instead, in the violet Alaskan evening daylight of "the parking lot field there," I mimed a gun-firing demonstration for Bob, as much as one can give a gun lesson when one has never fired a gun. I tried to mimic what the almost pathologically Relaxed Tone gun store salesman had showed me.

"What brand is it?" Bob asked, gingerly touching the stock as though expecting a shock.

"A Winchester (glancing at label to make sure) . . . no no, Remington 870" —870 of what, I wasn't certain.

Despite not being one of your big animal killers—not being one of your big anything killers—Bob at this stage probably knew as much about the human invention known as firearms as I did. Just from being around Alaskans for a couple of years. This was not for lack of research on my part. I had probably studied my choice of weapon more extensively than I had my choice of laptop or my place of shelter.

The early part of my research had not been auspicious. It had all started in Roger Longhenry's living room on a freezing April morning. Roger might have since left, but that didn't stop him from intentionally or unintentionally delivering my first couple of serious Step Two lessons, on the importance of firearms awareness.

"Er, I don't think you'd want to fire a shotgun that way," I remember him saying offhandedly as he looked for a particular Traffic song on the stereo. "Not if you want to keep your face."

For fun, I had been looking through the sights of Roger's weapon, with the stock up against the bridge of my nose sniper-style. I hadn't really even thought about Step Two yet. Winter was still raging. But I Free Ranged rather than admit more gratuitous Cheechakoness.

"I know that," I said, casually lowering the gun. "I was inspecting the grain." Actually, I hadn't even been completely sure it was a shotgun. It was just a large metal-and-wood gun. Not a pistol, of that I was sure.

"It's not loaded," Roger said from behind a glass of Baileys. "I don't even have any shells. I only have it out because I'm cleaning the basement. It's my sister-in-law's." Then he showed me how you're supposed to hold and fire a shotgun.

My second gun lesson also occurred at Roger's, about three days after my return from Barrow. It was the last time we hung out before he left Alaska. This time I was with JM, and in the interim since the previous visit, I had started thinking more practically about gathering my own food.

JM, who grew up eating things like hasenpfeffer and tripe, had of late been researching greenhouse possibilities and local potassium sources she could grow during Alaskan winters. She was willing to trade the roughage if I would shoot the protein. I had already started studying firearm types, and knew a fair amount more than I had during the earlier incident. I could tell a shotgun from a rifle, at least.

On our way out of Roger's house at the end of the visit, I saw the gun again, this time in the spare bedroom that becomes a junk storage center when a human lives in an entire house by him or herself. I picked it up to examine things like weight and gauge, and aimed it, relatively properly this time, at a coat hanger in the open closet separating the storage bedroom from the living room. The living room that contained, several inches away, things like television, VCR, and stereo with my Traffic tape in it.

Since Roger didn't "even have any shells," I truly almost fired a test shot, to see if I liked the "action" of what my research had by now confirmed was definitely a shotgun. About twelve milliseconds before I made this life-changing decision, perhaps prompted by some kind of instinctive Cheechako-alert, Roger walked by, popped his head in the room and said lightly, "Got the safety on? That thing's loaded."

The gun for which he so recently hadn't even owned shells was suddenly *loaded?*

Seems a particular moose had been harassing his dog Max, who bunked in a dog house outside, and now it was personal. So Lesson Number Two was "Never assume a gun is unloaded. This is how people die."

No one—not JM, not anyone—has ever known how close I came to reducing the number of rooms in Roger's house by one. I was abashed at how casually fate had allowed me to learn this rather crucial lesson. My arms were actually shaking as I laid the gun back down on the bed. In the car ride home JM just thought my shakiness was emotion over Roger's pending departure.

But once I recovered, these prototype Step Two events just reenergized me to really study my choice in mechanical propulsion of fiery lead. On my next few Costco toilet paper runs, I found myself frequenting the gun stores that sprout in Anchorage like burrito places do in San Francisco. I heard myself asking about things like safety features, bullet trajectory, and moose-incapacitating firepower range. (Any hunter worth his or her salt will tell you to hunt moose with a rifle, but since I would also be hunting birds and small game, I chose a weapon that would also work at short range on a moose until I could afford the proper weapon.)

This was possibly the worst time in American history to price firearms since the Boston Tea Party, given the Columbine shootings a few weeks earlier. Even most Western legislators were starting to consider limiting the number of antiaircraft Stingers one could buy over-the-counter per week to twelve.

But not one Alaskan proprietor so much as blinked when his or her rote "Can I help you?" greeting was answered with, "Yes. I'm in the market for a gun. Quickly." One of them, in fact, took me under his sourdough wing when he heard I had big plans to live a subsistence lifestyle in the Bush somewhere at some point.

So as the wildflowers were opening in 1999, my Step Two preparations were progressing. The last part of my early research had to do with discerning which animals were legal to hunt in which areas at which time. For this I consulted the extensive and impressively macabre *Alaska State Hunting Regulations* tome.

Some of the more memorable passages in this piece of literature include:

• *Take the skull and skin (with claws attached) of the bear you have killed from the kill site to an officially designated "sealing officer." The skull must be skinned from the hide and they must both be unfrozen.* (The author here has been influenced by Poe, I believe.)

• *If you kill a big game animal where the bag limit is restricted to one sex, you must keep enough of the sex organs (penis, scrotum, testicles, udder, teats, vaginal orifice) naturally attached to part of a rear quarter to show the sex of an animal.* (I'm surprised certain parental groups aren't trying to restrict the free publication's distribution based on that clause alone.)

And, my favorite, an eloquent piece about something mysterious on moose called brow tines:

• *In some areas, bulls with antlers less than 50 inches wide are legal if they have at least three brow tines on EITHER side. In other areas, bulls with antlers less than 50 inches wide must have at least four brow tines on*

Nobody Shoot, Nobody Get Hurt

EITHER side to be legal. . . . However, if the antlers are 50 or more inches wide, it doesn't matter how many brow tines are present.

* * * * *

The volume was not easy reading. It took me weeks and several calls to the Department of Fish and Game just to discern which Game Management Unit I lived in. By mid-June, what I learned from almost two month's study of the almost unbelievably technical and largely acronym-comprised 112-page text (evidently all hunters are expected to also be postdoctoral wildlife biologists and thesaurus readers), relieved me of any fantasy I had of hunting something substantive my first time out.

In July—which is when I was testing my gun on this expedition with Bob and Sunny—moose, caribou, dall sheep, grouse, ptarmigan, and most geese and ducks are off-limits. These are the things I could see myself eating. I like the way moose roast tastes, and I've always been a big fan of fowl, especially prepared *mu shu* style.

Technically, two black bear a year are legal to take. But I didn't want to shoot a bear. I can't explain why, other than to say that bears don't feel like prey to me. I'd heard mixed stories about the quality of the meat, but with moose plentiful on the Kenai Peninsula, some would say too plentiful, I didn't see why it was necessary to shoot a predator. It felt a little too much like fratricide. On several quite unintentional occasions, I've looked into a bear's eyes and have felt mutual understanding. Plus, I was still appreciative of the roving polar bear sparing me on my pack ice sprint. I'm convinced it was never more than a few yards from me. At times I felt I could smell its breath. It was seafoody.

The only other species you are apparently permitted to kill year-round is the snowshoe hare. Well, that and one special category the regulations encyclopedia calls "feral fowl." Evidently, in Game Management Units 15A through C, which include Homer, the lake

175

Not Really An Alaskan
Mountain Man

Odie was sending us to and the "the parking lot field there" where Bob and I were haphazardly packing, pheasants had escaped from people who had imported them to raise domestically (sort of like mail-order brides), and they had begun breeding successfully. You see the males posturing ridiculously all over downtown Homer. Pheasant males, too.

The Alaska Department of Fish and Game doesn't view Units 15A through C the way the State Department once viewed Ellis Island. Its decision makers want these pheasants eliminated with extreme prejudice as a foreign species, sort of like Cheechakos. They were thus open year-round without limit (which is indeed how many clutch-repairing auto mechanics look at Cheechakos).

I sort of liked the sound of the bureaucratic characterization "feral fowl." How insulting. "Kill the bastards," the regulations intimated in their subtle, techno-speak way.

So it was snowshoe hare or feral pheasant this time out. A moose was my real, eventual subsistence goal, simply for efficiency: one moose is a winter's worth of meat. The season for moose is the fall. Given my desire for some kind of relative familiarity with the shotgun, I was looking at this summer outing as a warm-up, a start to the training curve for stalking and eliminating with minimal prejudice a moose come September for my winter meat in the Kelvinator. Some small game would make a nice start, and a good meal.

＊ ＊ ＊ ＊ ＊

It was pushing a slightly diffuse 10:15 P.M. in the parking lot field there, and Bob wasn't satisfied with the scope of the AAA map he was scouring on the hood of my car.

"How far do you want to go in carrying that (gesturing to the firearm pointing up at the sky)?"

"The gun?"

"Yeah."

Nobody Shoot, Nobody Get Hurt

"Is it generally thought of as a burdensome accouterment?"

"I dunno. Is it? Maybe not. Do they have ergonomic standards for killing equipment yet?"

"As long as it doesn't backfire, it's OSHA-compliant for me."

Five minutes of silence ensued as we finished packing and then drummed a bit. Then I said, "The lake is something like six or eight miles in, I think Odie said. I don't know where the exact trailhead is, though."

"This is something we should take seriously," Bob said. "This map is not detailed at all." I chose not to mention to Bob that this was a recurring problem for me.

He handed me a heel of one of his girlfriend's special loaves of bread. Sunny the breathing vacuum cleaner pounced on a sizable crumb before it hit the ground. Having her along was more like it. I had learned that lesson at least. I was curious what type of a hunting dog she would prove to be. I already loved her unconditionally as a play-mate. Her biscuit quota was high as things stood. I had no idea how I'd reward an effective retriever.

"Look at these hills," Bob said, gazing around us at the splendor of the Kenai Peninsula backcountry. "They're purple. Let's get into them."

Before we did that, I took what felt like the dramatic step of Loading the Gun. At least I presumed I was loading it properly. With fumbling fingers I fed the shells in what seemed to be the direction for the hammer to strike something metallic. It was a remarkably easy motion. Almost obvious. Just like they showed me at the gun store.

But what if I was doing something wrong? My gun salesman had comforted me somewhat in explaining that much of the research and development in recreational firearms in the past half century has surrounded ensuring that dumb, drunken people don't accidentally hurt themselves. "The reason you have to pump the shell into the chamber that way is that if someone could do something stupid, he would," the nonliberal told me. I felt thankfulness to the Remington Company for its foresight.

Shotgun shells in the barrel, then. Three of them. Just to hear the words come out of my mouth, I commented to Bob, "Well, I guess we're . . . carrying a loaded firearm now."

"Okay," Bob consented, munching on a bread crust. But a question was working its way forward from his medulla. "Is that legal?"

"I have no idea. The hunting regulations are indecipherable."

"It should be, dammit," he asserted, slamming a tube of toothpaste on the hood of my car. "I know my Fourteenth Amendment."

* * * * *

We'd find out soon enough. Officialdom is what Bob, for the moment, was looking for, as he wanted to find out whether a detailed topographical map for the area we were traveling to was obtainable in the wilderness. At 11:00 on a Thursday/Friday/Saturday night. I had no argument with this. I knew the hassles of backcountry trekking without a good map.

We were armed with Odie's tip, and we knew we were close, but had no idea how to find her suggested lake. We knew it was south, toward Soldotna. Her shop was closed, so we couldn't even call her. Bob, having come from Homer to the south, indicated that the sport-fishing shops and diners in Cooper Landing might still be open, and we could inquire there. These, he recalled, were "about fifteen minutes" down the highway.

About fifteen feet down the highway, he pulled off into a dirt parking lot. I followed suit.

"Fifteen minutes, five seconds, what's the difference?" I asked of my gun safety spotter and navigator, as we popped into Hamilton's Cafe Lounge, two shaggy hunters after hours with determined looks on our faces and breadcrumbs on our lips.

Nobody Shoot, Nobody Get Hurt

At the threshold, I had a moment of concern about waltzing into a place that had all the dim-lit, Lite Beer looks of not exactly being . . . shaggy-friendly, just to ask for directions to a nebulous trailhead. Particularly when one shaggy man had a lupine blossom from the other side of the bay in the brim of his slightly too-foreign Tilley hat. I had made the switch from the Marcos mask in mid-June.

But we bonded immediately on the subject of guns with the septuagenarian bartender Charlie and the one drinker in Hamilton's on this night, who set about doing the job of the armchair outdoorsman by scaring us into trembling wrecks about bears.

"You heard about the fellow."

We had. Everybody had. The fellow was a celebrity. We were in fact headed into an area not far from where a brown bear ate the fellow a month earlier. Actually, she took a bite and then decided she didn't like him; didn't savor the flavor. Unfortunately, the bite was out of the fellow's head, and well, despite the evidence of the Reagan cabinet, one needs a head.

The finicky bear was still at large, though presumably Fish and Wildlife enforcement officers were after her for a littering violation. I choose my gender pronoun because those sows protecting their cubs, they can be . . . protective.

"Better bring a twelve-gauge shotgun," the customer, who I think might have been a member of the Cooper Landing Fire Department, judging by his walkie-talkie labeled COOPER LANDING FIRE DEPARTMENT and his hat reading CLFD, advised.

"Got one o' those," I confirmed, spitting out an imaginary hunk of chaw on the rug. After twenty-nine years of life, I finally had the right answer for that kind of suggestion.

We were amongst friends in Hamilton's, that much was relievingly clear. Step Two was in the air, and that was *aarigaa*.

Our only danger was a particularly rural one: there was no way to politely extract ourselves from the conversation until Charlie was done visiting with us. Never mind that it was after 11:00 P.M. and we were two strangers. After a few minutes, I began to stop wanting to extract myself. I think Bob felt the same way. The whole scene was giving us a powerfully healthy sense of "the more things change, the more they stay the same."

Charlie had lived in Homer in the early 1970s, and the soap operas he described making lives interesting back then sounded extremely familiar. Different names. Same patterns of primate behavior.

Beer kept flowing. With the smiling gentleness that comes from years of realizing only smiling gentleness makes points, Charlie began expostulating on popular Alaskan subjects ranging from the increase in land seizure since the Reagan Era to the best solution to the spruce beetle infestation. After about forty minutes in the vortex of Hamilton's Cafe Lounge, I felt so comfortable that I thought I'd try to get some tips about the local Step Two climate.

"Any hares in this here foresT?" I asked, wiping my lips on my sleeve. I had started taking on quite a country twang. It blended with my Iñupiaq consonants. Out of the corner of my eye, I thought I saw Bob's mouth forming into a little O.

"Oh yeah, lots of hare," Charlie said slowly, and the firefighter chimed in happily, "Bursting with hare. You'll see hare all over the place."

"Any feral fowl?"

"Any feral whatsis?"

"Er, feral fowl."

"Nah. The grocery store's down in Soldotna."

"No, I mean pheasant and such."

Charlie and the firefighter caught eyes. "There are no pheasant in Alaska, son," the bartender said.

"But in the regula . . . ah, forget it. I must've been mistaken." A tremendous amount of Academy Award-winning Free Ranging would

Nobody Shoot, Nobody Get Hurt

be necessary for a shaggy Cheechacko to sound like a hunting authority in Cooper Landing. So it was hare then.

"OK," I reminded myself. "So it isn't a bowhead or even a moose. You gotta start somewhere." That was becoming my mantra.

As a veteran of a 48-ton whale—both its weight and aggressiveness had been consistently increasing during some monumental Free Ranging sessions at the Down East Saloon—I was sure that something as personal-sized as a snowshoe hare would all but leap onto my plate, fully skewered and cooked.

* * * * *

Armed with the information provided by the topo map Charlie eventually got around to pulling out from behind the bar, we staggered out of Hamilton's into a fading purple world at a quarter to midnight.

"Wellup," I said, hitching up my pants, "We'd best go shoot dinner. (Looking up at the sky.) Or breakfast."

I hopped in the Subaru, got licked by my dog, and popped in the Allman Brothers. I was feeling very rural. We found our trailhead without effort. Then there was a slight complication in that we had to deal with a federal sign-in kiosk in order to get into the federal trees of the Kenai wilderness. It made both of us nervous.

We had some difficult questions to answer on the entrance form. We debated these at length in hushed voices, particularly what to list under the "planned activities" column. We finally decided to include, "talking, listening, and relaxing." We left out "hunting" in case I winged anything or anyone unintentionally. We parked near the trailhead.

"Ah, another place still breathing," I sighed as we went through the last-minute ritual of jettisoning the TP and other frills from our packs: no matter how much I unloaded, I was overpacked. In killing equipment alone. My gun kept slipping off my shoulder, and my fishing rod jutted about eight feet into the air on the left side of my pack like a radio antenna.

I, though, was feeling it there at the trailhead for the excursion to what we were by now calling Odie's Lake. In this kind of situation (a clear Alaskan summer midnight), the forest feels like it's calling to you. You can hear it, and not just with your ears. The very air precipitates a sensation of low gravity and high oxygen.

For several minutes I was confused about what to do with my car key. It was one of the few keys left in my life. Spruce and cottonwood were the dominant vegetation, and I considered a treasure map and key burial under one of them. This was an option I very luckily rejected. Instead I stuck the key in my pack and triple checked the zipper. I was already losing the sense of linear time we carry around for most of life, and I didn't trust myself to think about locks of any kind for as long as it took to hunt a meal.

Judging by the circular dance and karate kicks Bob was doing next to me as he finished packing and unpacking, he too felt the simultaneously confusing and relaxing dynamic of wilderness that makes you wonder how Gregorian Time got invented. The danger here, again, was being so at one with the place that you forgot that this was subarctic wilderness, where almost anything can happen. Like head-chomping bears bidding you good evening.

"Did I just say that, or think it?" I asked Bob of the danger-of-beauty thought.

"Do you feel like you said it?" he asked.

In what seemed an amazing testimonial to the general rightness of the hunting mission, after more than two hours organizing, Bob and I hoisted our packs onto our backs and slammed our motorized vehicle doors shut at the same second, which was also the exact instant Sunny emitted her first "Let's do it" holler. She took off into the trees after her echo. It was 11:59 P.M., according to Bob's watch, when we started the tromping ruckus unique in nature to humans. Thursday, I think.

Nobody Shoot, Nobody Get Hurt

* * * * *

We could hear the salmon-clogged Russian River below us in the for-est. Fiery magenta clouds were collecting in chaotic swirls above distant mountains like black light coronas. Quite fortunately there appeared to be only one trail leading from the parking meadow. Stepping across a small waterfall, which placed us ankle deep in little dewy stars of dwarf dogwood, we proceeded to hike through the night, solemnly chanting a song by Coolio as bear deterrent.

Usually I wake up and the world is covered with dew. I'd never got-ten dewy overnight with the wildflowers before. I felt the sense of head-ing vaguely east, to meet the new day.

When we tired of Coolio we made loud chimpanzee sounds of the "warning another group" variety, gleaned from years of nature docu-mentary watching. This went on so long I was beginning to forget English. In fact, the hike continued without break until, guided by bluebell nightlights, we found the lake roughly the advertised eight miles in at about 4:10 A.M. "What a cakewalk finding the Halibut Cove lake would be at this time of year," I thought, although that would somewhat preclude skating on it. Anyway, fate had different plans. We had found a new gorgeous lake. We had found Odie's Lake.

I knew this was the case because of a high-pitched war whoop far in front of me that snapped me out of my nervous gun safety mum-bling ("When the red's not showing, that means the safety's on," I had been explaining to the rhythm of the trail). The shout was so piercing after the forest's nighttime whispers and so different from our chimp song that it set me sprinting clumsily ahead along the path to rescue my friend from the bear's jaws.

My gun and sword were clanging against my over-heavy pack. I lumbered and stumbled along this way until an overhanging tree limb obligingly launched me skyward by way of a fishing pole vault. I landed hard and it took me a couple of moments to right myself. When

Not Really
/\ An Alaskan
Mountain Man

I caught up to a nail-filing Bob around a switchback, he was looking down on a mist-shrouded, mountain-encircled hourglass that steamed below us like a good witch's brew.

It was a perfectly still body of water, other than the circular evidence of insects. A coyote yipped just above us on a hillside. Just then, Sunny, a bit of celestial sweat on her snout, bounded out of the hills on our left and timed her first ecstatic leap into Odie's Lake. She disappeared, then emerged from behind a curtain of mist, causing a Thai shadow theater performance in the shimmery liquid shadows. The show's ripples cycled rapidly in the lake, like an out-of-control silent film projector. We just sat watching this feature in silence.

"This the place?" Bob finally asked.

"This is *the* place," I confirmed. I was sucking blood out of my thumb from wild rose thorn wounds sustained in my rescue attempt. The lake looked like a pot of steaming soup.

"Did you say that or just think it?" Bob asked. "About the soup."

"I'm not sure, did it sound like I said it?"

Another long, maybe ten-minute spate of symphonic silence followed. Now it was just a question of finding the right place to camp. Hunting was to begin in the morning. The glowing bluebells led us like votive candles as we stomped in waterlogged boots, and everything around us drank in the early morning dampness. Even Sunny had muddy ankle socks as she led the way.

And in fact like a dog circling a potential bed before deciding it deserves plopping down on, we moved more or less in a loop around the accessible part of the lake. Finally, at 4:40, we came upon a secret moose path that hadn't been there the previous time we'd passed.

This route turned out to take us up to a relatively dry elevated meadow for our morning's sleep. Our campsite was just within view of the billions of expanding Doppler effects on the water below. There were only a few dozen stars out above our clearing, and the air was thick with the special damp perfume that wild rose petals emit just before dawn in July.

The next twenty minutes passed in a near dream, with alternately warm and cool air currents washing over my face that were strongly suggestive of nearby glaciers. Somehow my ancient tent got set up. We stashed our food, theoretically out of bear reach. While we made camp, a waterfall that would guide us the next day crescendoed into the dominant player in the white noise summer symphony. Because of a gently twisting breeze, it was hard to tell which direction the waterfall was— the effect was like Surround Sound.

* * * * *

Oh, but fleetingly visit my moments of living in the now. At around 4:55, while I was unloading the last of my gear and a gentle wind was singing me a lullaby, I noticed the smell. The fishy smell, to be specific. Just as I was ready to allow myself some deep relaxation, too. How Good I Had It a Moment Ago Syndrome had again reared its head.

It was my detachable daypack, reeking at ten yards. Right. I had meant not to bring that. There was no mistaking it: it was fresh seafood essence, from an outing the previous week. Something like 112 pounds of Kachemak Bay halibut were at the moment leaking out of my bulging freezer, to supplement the whale smell in my cabin, which was just starting to fade.

I held aloft the stinking piece of gear, thinking about the fellow again. Thanks to our time at Hamilton's Cafe Lounge, I was no longer cocky about the "gentle" brown bears as I had been with JM on our kayaking trip. Comfortably certain that bears like fish, and cursing their annoyingly acute sense of smell, I was getting that periodic "At what point is it too dangerous to even be outside?" feeling. Anyone who has heard strange sounds outside his or her tent in the wilderness in the middle of the night knows what I'm talking about. Nowhere to hide.

Hotels sounding like a fabulous development for the species. Severe self-recrimination at one's environmental inclinations. And there really was a fellow-killer on the loose.

The tingling terror wasn't as acute as it had been on my snowmachine on the pack ice, but it was definitely genuine Cheechako fear. If anything, I think the sensation was exacerbated, or possibly even entirely caused by the fact that I now had an ostensible means of defending myself, and thus no excuse if mauled. Ugh. Classic Cheechako way to die: brand new gun beside your partially chewed corpse. As I stashed the effervescent daypack with our food, I was already embarrassed for me.

The Free-Range grapevine had it that the fellow who got crunched by the brown bear here on the peninsula was armed and in fact had emptied his rifle into the animal, with the effect of a powerfully delivered insult. He was, judging from the Cooper Landing firefighter's scoff, carrying a weapon of regionally insufficient caliber. Being armed had no effect, or possibly a detrimental effect. Who knows whether the sow would've attacked if the fellow hadn't wounded/annoyed her?

When I was just an unarmed hiker, non-polar bears had never really been a problem for me. This, of course, could just have been luck. I might have met nice bears, the way that some travelers are fortunate enough to run across nice people. I wondered how I would be able to tell a convicted fellow-eater from a friendlier specimen. Suddenly our meadow seemed like a dangerously exposed and poorly chosen site. I had the lurking sense of being watched.

As the gun-bearer, I felt it was my duty to guard our group. I don't know who made up this rule, but I felt it every moment the darn shotgun was slung on my shoulder. Add to that my aforementioned lack of interest in shooting a bear at all, and my spirit wasn't at peace as the 5:00 A.M. hour rolled around. Come September, if it were a bear and me, in the wild, dueling for my just-killed moose, that might be a different story. I'd have a reason. Step Two. Bear or me. But for now, my goal was mutual respect.

Nobody Shoot, Nobody Get Hurt

I sighed a nervous sigh and looked over my gear. The fellow's macabre end had me wondering things like, does the shampoo in my hair attract Ursidae? (The commercials implied it's a lure for any member of the opposite sex, of any species.) What about the coagulated blood between my fingers? The previous day's sushi sweating out of me? Space Age fibers never really washed since whaling? Bob's girlfriend's honey-tinged bread? Man, at that moment even an ignition-free snowmachine felt like an unimaginable luxury.

My one consolation was that no mammal other than my own species had thus far shown a predilection for Polysorbate 80, again my principal sustenance in the field. But this redeeming feature of my "come and get me" smell wasn't quite good enough to put my mind at ease at our hunting camp site. I was suddenly feeling like the hunted. Finally, I could stand it no longer. I pulled out my toothbrush and waved it like a wand. "Is it the saccharine in the toothpaste the experts believe the bears are attracted to?" I yelled toward Bob in a fairly hysterical manner. "Or is it the minty Tartar Control freshness?"

"It's the T25, I believe," Bob called back, wiping some recent bear scat off his boot on a fern near my tent. He had nothing to worry about. He was defenseless.

I watched Sunny madly digging for something in the grass surrounding my pack. She was also feeling no fear. I guess I alone had to carry the burden of the gun-toter. I felt like Frodo with the Ring.

I tried to route my thoughts elsewhere, as the new day's light became more authoritative. Waterfalls. Step Two. I unloaded the shotgun for sleep-safety reasons (utilizing the knowledge I had gained during Roger Lesson Number 2). But this motion only reminded me that beyond parole-violating bears, I was a little nervous about the true purpose of this expedition. The gorgeous hike had left me further concerned that my normal wilderness intent—to be in sync with the ecosystem around me—might be threatened by my new, stated violent mission. The subsistence rightness I felt in Barrow seemed a long time ago.

But just as I started to list my rote Step Two rationalizations about the benefits of healthy, wild meat, the world took a palpably deep pre-sunrise sigh and my emotions shifted with it. Like a pacified infant, I watched in awe as a bee half the size of my fist flew by in a sonic-flanged maelstrom to take care of some nearby business.

I took a deep whiff of wild rosebud. I exhaled for about thirty seconds. "This is the time for small fires with hot cores and perhaps some quiet drumming," I reevaluated. Bob wholeheartedly agreed, possibly because he sensed that he might be faced with a Cheechako freakout, very far from the nearest mental health facility.

Drowsy thrushes, deeply involved in their own culture, at first objected cordially in the meadow around us, before getting into the rhythm of our music. Sunny joined in with howls, her snout pointing at the sky. The coyotes seemed into it as well. I have always found them to have a very open-minded society.

When we stopped drumming, the universe had diminuendoed another click, as if in preparation for the day that was soon to explode. Our speaking voices got louder like the sound of a late-night radio as soon as the light's turned off. Bob, Sunny, and I talked and joked around a cottonwood blaze like three folks recently admitted to heaven.

The fire popped and snapped, catching the chrome on my gun. When 5:30 A.M. paid a visit, I climbed into the tent next to my dog, who was a curled wet pumpkin. She was hardly moving a muscle as she looked up at me and blinked. As I zipped my sleeping bag, I remembered the Leavitts. How easy the hunt had been for their minds. Then I briefly thought of city traffic and the fluorescent-lit chain stores in Anchorage. God, was that just this evening? Do all these things exist in the same world?

I fell asleep immersed in rose vapors, wondering if I would kill when I awoke.

Chapter 8
The Shots Not Heard
'round the Forest

We knew the coming day would wake us in a few hours, but Bob, Sunny, and I welcomed the sunlight that flushed us from our tents. Indeed, it felt tropical this mid-morning, even in the shade. The sun was actually hot on my face at 9:00 A.M. I smeared some chemicals on my nose to make it not burn. Sunny, accustomed to a mild-to-frigid Southcentral Alaska, was confused. I saw her panting and lapping up dew puddles that had gathered on our ground tarp.

After breakfasting, the three of us meandered through the forest to a stream feeding Odie's Lake to fill our water bottles. It took about five minutes of bushwhacking to reach the lake itself. While Bob filled his bottle, I wandered off toward an accessible bank, and found a small meadow that a bear had very obviously used as a bed-and-breakfast the previous night. After waking, it had presumably moved on, upon finishing its toilette nearby. I looked for traces of human being in its leavings, but found only fish bones. This encouraged me as I looked out over the water. I could see perfect imprints of the surrounding mountain snowfields taking a dip in the lake.

Feeling the urge to submerge, I peeled off my shirt and jeans and belly flopped into the lake to join the reflections, climbing out seven invigorating seconds later. There's something about forty-degree glacial runoff that makes you forget all your worries. Even your gun worries. All you remember is what a beautiful planet houses you. And what a fulfilling gift your (shocked and shivering) senses are.

"*Aarigaa*," I screamed. Half a second later, the echo agreed. Half a second after that, Bob concurred as well, with a war whoop from somewhere out of sight.

189

Not Really
An Alaskan
Mountain Man

The meadow moss and flowers felt nice on my feet as I drip-dried, so I lay down Goldilocks-style in the mushed grass of the bear bed with my pack as a pillow. Sunny joined me, and I untangled a necklace of rose braids from her sopping neck. She curled up in the body circle that always makes me admire her spinal design. In ten seconds she was asleep against my hip. Sunny has two gears: fifth and park. I relaxed even further on the grounds that if she didn't smell a bear, there must not be one nearby.

* * * * *

Fifteen minutes later, I scrambled along the lakeshore, sundried and armed to the teeth, to find Bob meditating. I sat and we mulled over the Adaptionist evolution topic a little, as we had agreed the night before. He wondered if chromosomes can learn. I speculated that perhaps the ever-expanding generation gap was evidence that we as a species are moving beyond physicality and into pure consciousness. High, wispy clouds were like dendrites above us. Sunny had wandered off into some lakeside weeds.

I mention all this early morning conversation and swimming because I was observing that in the first few waking hours of our hunting trip, not a whole heck of a lot of hunting was going on. I tried to rationalize that we were warming up.

A fish about five feet into the lake leaped as if shocked. "Do they make nature like this anymore?" I asked Bob. He shook his head. Sitting with the gun on my lap, I spent a few minutes scrawling words in my notebook. Finally I looked up. "So, you want to hunt?"

"Sure," Bob consented. Neither one of us moved.

"What sort of terrain do jackrabbits like?" he asked rather flatly after a while.

"Snowshoe hares," I corrected.

"Snowshoe hares."

The Shots Not Heard 'round the Forest

"I don't know. They drink, I guess. So, near water?"

"Wanna head up toward that waterfall then?" Bob asked, pointing vaguely to the sound that had been directionally confusing us since we arrived.

"Good idea," I said, slinging on my gun.

"Which way do you think that is? South?"

"For now," I explained to him, and gave a brief primer on my brush with the pending polar reversal. Then a thought occurred to me. "Say, do you know how to gut a hare, if I . . . er, land one?"

"Can't be too hard," he said, glancing at the sword bungeed on my pack. "They have pretty much the same organs we do. Slice belly to bowel, stick the foot in your pocket."

Sunny reappeared dramatically and interrupted our discussion by getting into a shouting match with a beautiful shorebird called a yellowlegs. The bird drew Bob's focused attention for several minutes. He crept close to the lake's edge and stared at it. I wondered what he was looking at. Then he came back and commented on the relative fuel consumption necessary to propel a migrating shorebird 6,700 miles versus that to fly a human to Cancun.

"They do with a few worms what takes us a monster pile of steel, digital navigation equipment, and troughs of jet fuel to do," he observed. Then he added, "So. I guess let's go kill something."

It was great to have this kind of a conscience along on such an important day for me. But after ten more minutes of such conversation, I felt we might be on the verge of procrastinating. It had to be close to noon. On what I thought might be Friday. I didn't know exactly how one starts hunting, as opposed to just hiking. Was there a particular stalking pose? My only reference point was Elmer Fudd, who never seemed to have much success.

* * * * *

Not Really An Alaskan
Mountain Man

Bob and I split up for a bit as we would do several times during the day. I sensed he would want to leave the actual killing to me, and I wanted to give him the opportunity to be away from the carnage. This was my mission, my little step in the Alaskan coming-of-age game. And he had been nice enough to come along and supervise. I just hoped he stayed in hearing range in case anything went wrong.

Bob laced his boots, then got up and started toward the trees. From inside the forest canopy, my human friend announced that he was going to start up the willow-lined slope toward the waterfall. I told him I'd join him in a few minutes. To let him get out of range. Once he left, I whistled the *Pink Panther* theme to keep bears aware of my exact location. Then I stood up, breathed deeply, and stretched loudly. The trail beckoned. It was time for Step Two.

Sunny and I felt the sense of total aloneness that a healthy forest can give a guy and his dog. Sensing the Event, her fun meter humming at full blast, she was sticking close to me. I ritualistically reloaded the gun with the same shells that I had removed before going to sleep. I hooked on my pack and grabbed my gun. We reached the forest canopy under the world's most perfect weather: seventy degrees and glacially breezy.

I rested my right pointer on the safety. I readied my left palm on the pump. I molded my face into a concentrating expression. I pointed the gun down at the ground, for safety reasons. Then I shouldered the gun, as the stalking posture left me no free hands and was too unwieldy, what with my heavy pack. I couldn't see skulking around the forest all day like that.

"This is it," I thought when I had sorted out the ergonomics. "I am hunting." I could feel that the moment had arrived. I didn't feel indigenous, so much as scared, and maybe a little bit exhilarated. But how can I separate this from the general exhilaration of being in the Alaskan wilderness on an endless summer day? Maybe the difference was the intense

The Shots Not Heard 'round the Forest

"this is real" feeling one gets in one's belly when taking the leap and engaging in something that one knows is a monumental step in one's life—like a wedding, or switching credit cards to get free air miles. But I didn't have much time to think about this as I stepped into the forest.

Three mystical strides in, Sunny took off like a bolt and flushed a hare from the willows in a trajectory directly in front of me. An open shot at twelve yards. It was unfathomably good luck. I unslung the gun with a dramatic shoulder shake and had almost leveled it (as per Roger Lesson Number 1) at what had once been the serpentining form of the hare, before it was lost in the trees. I'm not sure I ever quite got the safety off, but I pressed at it to make sure it was on again in case I had. "Wow," I thought. "The whole hunting business sure comes and goes quickly."

I was surprised to see that the hare had been tannish brown, like the forest floor. I forgot that the snowshoes switch back from the white winter coat they had been wearing the last few times I'd seen them, including while Driving While Happy with JM after escaping from Halibut Cove in December.

"All right, all right," I murmured. "All in all, not a bad start." I had been startled into an awareness of how real this really was. This wasn't a dress rehearsal. This was dinner. I looked up into the forest at my amazing dog, who was still in pursuit. She was yelling joyously. Now I felt a little bit indigenous.

I didn't at first realize how Sunny knew to flush what was pretty much the only legal animal to hunt in Southcentral Alaska at this time of year. She had spent her puppyhood in suburbia just like I had spent my puppyhood in suburbia. Initially I thought it was just luck. But later in the summer Tosha, an often-barefoot, eleven-year-old neighbor of mine, took to bringing her bunny Oreo over to my cabin when she biked around Fritz Creek in the afternoons. The terrified animal, thrust into the confusing world of golden retriever mixes and zydeco music, always promptly hopped under my deck. Sunny would spend the time with her bottom sticking out of the suspected warren, singing. She evidently has a primeval urge to go after Leporidae. Live and learn. Turns out her performance with the hare was, genetically, the moment she had been waiting for. Not unlike a Leavitt at whaling season or a Roger Longhenry with a chainsaw. I made a mental note to add this point in my conversation with Bob about Adaptionist evolution.

After a few seconds spent processing what had just happened, I realized there was more to this. Sunny was telling me the hunt wasn't over. I stormed off the trail after her, following the hare into the hilly brush. And I tripped over a root almost immediately.

It was a good thing I had checked the safety. Once again I guiltily gave thanks that there were no witnesses to my parody of Mountain Man activities. There are just too many things to trip over in Alaska. I pulled my face out of a rose patch and limped back to the trail, my mind reeling, the blood coursing and thumping in my temple. The prey got away. The animals in the forest, overall, seemed a lot smarter than their cultures are often given credit for in lab experiments.

I caught up with Bob after a series of hoots and breathlessly told him of the hare encounter, leaving out the details about the root slip and not even getting the hare in my sights. This is Free Ranging by Omission. Very common.

"I didn't hear a shot," he said, quite factually.

I laughed. Yes. Technically, I would have to fire a shot in order to bag a meal. I wasn't going to knife a snowshoe hare. As we worked our way along the trail (Bob keeping me and the gun barrel in front), I spent some moments in mimed contemplation of the ready position, so I could be prepared to fire when the next source of protein leaped across our path.

I was a reenergized Step Two radical. I watched every sprig for movement. I lay every footfall down softly and slowly. I began to wish I hadn't had the image of Elmer Fudd so firmly implanted in my childhood. Every twenty seconds I glanced behind me to make sure the footsteps I heard were Bob's and not the fellow-eating bear's.

Still sweating from the thrill of the hunt ten minutes later, I put down my pack and gun and took a swig of glacial runoff. The forest around us was almost completely dry already, except for the occasional glint of dew remaining from the early morning's aquaculture, cradled delicately within bluebell cups. The moistness of 4:00 A.M. felt like a great secret that had been shared with us.

I called to Sunny from wherever she had hightailed it into the hills. She was still after the hare it was my end of the bargain to shoot. When she trotted up, her tongue dragging along the ground, I gave her tons of pets. She was too excited to take a drink. For a few moments we just sat panting next to each other, looking back toward the spot where we last saw our dinner dart away.

✳ ✳ ✳ ✳ ✳

When I caught my breath, I found I wasn't just thirsty from the brief but promising hunt, I was famished. If there's one thing I knew about hunting, it's that it's not about the hunting. It's about the lunch break. Leaning against the protected trailside alcove over which the glacier runoff was trickling, I offered Bob some Polysorbate 80 I had fished out of my pack.

"I guess I'll have a little bit, as though that makes it less of a sin," he said, reaching into the heavily scented bag.

We resumed movement, and were steadily climbing now.

"I know, jerky is gross," I agreed. "But why a sin, other than the obvious, the premise itself? I even tried to buy the most natural kind this time—all-white-meat turkey." I shuddered at the memory of the beef hearts JM had tricked me into eating across the bay. I'd moved upscale in the purchase of dry, salted flesh. Even Sunny would eat this stuff.

For Bob, it was the premise itself. "It's not necessary. There are turkeys somewhere in, what . . ."

I looked down at the package. "Oregon."

"Oregon, crammed in some kind of heinous pen, pumped with who knows what . . . ." He wasn't raising his voice. Just speaking the truth.

"You're right of course," I said. "That's why I'm armed, right? I want this to be the last time for this . . ." I made the grimace the taste called for. It was like pasty dirt.

"It's not just the jerky. . . ." He said this very distractedly. He looked around and seemed to scan the hills, like he'd rather be discussing something else.

I, however, was focused. "So what do you think is the way to live and eat then?" I asked in a voice tinged with a bit of melodrama. "What are the options?"

"Well," Bob said contemplatively, "There was once a hunter/gatherer way to live, a natural way for us to be here, but because of the current system and the way food is manufactured, I'd say the most humane way now is probably to be vegan, I guess."

"OK, so jerky aside, what's your take on this hunt?" I inquired, stumbling on a protruding rock and nearly falling into a ninety-foot canyon.

He put his hand on my pack to steady me. "Not sure it's necessary."

I felt something rising in me, other than polysorbate indigestion. Something visceral, something primeval.

"I *am* that hunter/gatherer," I asserted, turning to face him and squeezing at my rib cage where the cereal commercials dare you to "pinch an inch." Bob ducked out of the way of my fishing rod. "I'm the same guy. Same genes. Same fight-or-flight mechanism. And I'm supposed to live and act as though I'm not because of something called a *system?* This is how I'm designed. It's as natural when I land a moose as when a . . . a lion lands a gazelle."

We huffed and puffed up the trail in silence for a few minutes, both reflecting on the sheer maudlin quality of my pontificating in the wilderness.

The Shots Not Heard 'round the Forest

"I can see that," Bob said finally, nodding. This is a man who can cook a nutritionally-complete stir-fry from weeds that grow behind his cabin. A guy who by nature would never consider buying 98 percent of what television spends a lot of money to convince our demographic are necessary products and ideas. "Within reason you want to live off the land. No domestication of animals."

Despite my invective, I was still working this out in my own heart. I stopped in my tracks, looked down at the forged steel and polished wood on my shotgun, and my train of thought trailed off. Could I stalk an animal that is minding its own business, and mangle its flesh, or not? As though on psychic autopilot, this same, rather essential question kept asking itself, ever since Laura's paralyzed moose story. Would I have really pulled the trigger on that first hare? What the hell was all this last-minute wavering? Had I learned nothing in the last seventeen months since coming to Alaska? In my mind at that moment, I was as much a Cheechako refugee as I ever was. I was back in my own yard, a broken chainsaw in my hands.

Just then Bob touched my shoulder and pointed behind me. He had caught sight of four moose in a flower-filled field slanting away below us, at thirty yards. The group included one possibly harvestable bull for this unit according to what the author of the brow tine description in the Alaska Hunting Regulations believes I should instinctively understand. I wished I hadn't left the hunting regulations tome on top of the Kelvinator. I could use its *I-Ching*-like random wisdom at this moment.

Sunny couldn't sense the vegans because we were upwind on a trail lined with grass five-and-a-third Sunnys tall. So we had some moments of quiet observation. I greeted the moose the way that came naturally: as friends. "In September though," I reflected, "they will be potential meals. How . . . weird." It depended on the moment. Just the way a polar bear or nature itself may look at me, I suppose.

The moose were suddenly aware of us but, judging from their continuing to munch, not overly alarmed. Perhaps they were cognizant of the regulations. My mind of course thrust the memory of the Groucho moose mom and calf into prominent focus at this moment. I sighed, remembering how sure I'd felt about subsistence on the North Slope pack ice. Where was Margaret when I needed her, convincing me in her nonchalance that this was absolutely the way it was supposed to be?

"Can't I be just another animal doing right by this place and being done right?" I wondered. "Just eating with appreciation and without remorse?" I couldn't believe guilt had to be associated with Step Two. Although when I thought about it, I myself wouldn't like to be shot, eviscerated, and eaten. "Man," I thought, looking at eight hundred pounds of meat, minimum. "If I did drop one of these, what would I do from there? I'm ten miles from my car."

But what an easy shot. I leveled the gun at the bull below us to see if I could do that. I could. At the same time, I was now sure that I could not from this distance discern his exact number of brow tines.

"How many, er, brow tines does that older bull have?" I whispered to Bob.

"Four. No six, maybe?" he guessed, squinting.

"Well, I think one of those answers makes it legal, the other illegal."

Maybe, I thought hopefully, the moose's lack of fear indicated that they were willing to sacrifice one of their own for our well-being, or maybe they were just unaware of what technology allowed us to do from this distance. That was just the dynamic JM and I discovered when we were momentarily thrust into subsistence across the bay back in December, without weapons. I preferred to consider the former. I thought of the breaching whales' message to the whaling captain, slightly revised.

It's okay, Cheechako. One moose is sustainable.

* * * * *

The Shots Not Heard 'round the Forest

Bob grabbed another piece of Polysorbate 80, breaking my moose contemplation spell and finishing off the package. "You are what you eat," he said with a brief smile, which melted into a gag as the smoke flavor invaded his taste buds.

"Convenient? Much appreciated? Light? Inexpensive?"

"Tasty and high in protein, too," he conceded, making a great effort to swallow. "Dehydrating meat was definitely an advancement for humans."

I thought about that one for a minute, peeling a pungent rose petal from my cheek, and finally exhorting heaven with my throat tight and my voice wavering, "Why'd they have to go and add the Polysorbate 80 in the first place?"

Bob thought about that one for about one-third of a second.

"Because someone invented the chemistry."

"Ah, because there was something to sell."

"Yeah. The marketing rep said, 'Hey, you want this chemical? You won't need to have some insurance risk minding the kiln on overtime for twenty hours a day. Fewer staff. Lower liability.'" Bob absent-mindedly reached into his small daypack, pulled out some Safeway Muenster Cheese, and handed me a wedge.

"Is this necessary?" I asked, digging in.

We both cracked up as the images of the Wisconsin cows, the freon refrigeration, and the jet fuel involved in bringing us the cheese came into clearer focus. Safeway brand, no less. Bob was raising the pertinent issues, I felt, the issues I deep down wanted raised. Yes, I would like to eat locally, rather than from some kind of Portland turkey concentration camp. If I bring jerky with me into the woods I want it to be from wild meat I harvest and smoke in my own smokehouse, with no polysorbates added at all. I'd learned that lesson back at Halibut Cove. A smokehouse was indeed high on my list of things to build. I just wasn't there yet.

And it was an expensive journey I was making, too. Subsistence would keep me working for wages until the initial fixed costs had been defrayed (boat, weapons, propane freezer, vacuum sealer). In the meantime, though, I was already spending more, pound for pound, to explore subsistence than I would to buy, say, a few hundred Odie's turkey sandwiches.

✶ ✶ ✶ ✶ ✶

Fixed costs aside, the "Is Step Two Necessary?" conversation wound up reinvigorating me, and I "hunted" energetically for about half an hour. Meaning, Sunny and I looked around for hares on a beautiful ridgeline trail. We kept at it until I felt a patch of wild celery nettles shooting microscopic effusions of poison into my arms. I hopped around and slapped myself in agony (which only made it worse).

I recovered after a few minutes. Bob was still keeping me and any shotgun scatter ahead of himself on the trail. A strong breeze was picking up. And after a full day of attempted subsistence, I was finding it hard to maintain my concentration. So passed another hour, my desire to kill fluctuating every fifteen minutes or so.

I was alone close to 4:15 P.M., blowing bubbles with my lips as I trekked lackadaisically forward. Bob had stopped to tie his boot a while back and was far behind, sauntering. Sunny was off on a private foray somewhere. I looked up. The alpine universe came together in a sloping feminine crease made mature with a nearby patch of wildflowers that were trembling. I felt like singing; it was a feeling that reminded me of the In Sync With Everything moment on Chainsaw Initiation Day. I held off bursting into song, however, as this tends to scare away prey; it tends to scare away animals of all species. Time slowed for a moment.

At this instant, the second hare appeared. This time I was ready for him and he wasn't for me. I was both quiet and downwind of my prey. He was just sitting there, a hare unaware, munching in a little dandelion garden. Not even covered up, he was completely exposed like a Cheechako on the pack ice. I leveled the gun, brought a shell into the chamber as silently as possible, and flicked the safety off. My fingers quivered around the stock for a few seconds. I started to creep a few steps closer. And . . . I didn't pull the trigger.

Sure, I was frightened to death about the potential effects on my shoulder of that motion. But the gun wasn't why I held off firing. The cause wasn't even the "Is Hunting Necessary and Kind?" debate. Rather it was the largish pile of fresh brown bear scat into which I stepped at this moment. I skidded and nearly fell, and said, "Whoa…" loudly as I steadied myself. From about the distance one could spit a hunk of Polysorbate 80, the hare darted away.

I thought of the animal that had left the steaming deposit. It couldn't have been more than a half hour earlier. Naturally my mind went to the worst-case individual. I took the incident to be a message from the fugitive bear, meaning, "Listen, fellow, why not hunt when it's really for your food, after you learn the skills, and not as some kind of hubristic test?"

I thought that sounded like a fair suggestion. Given that another bear had chosen, by a matter of minutes, to avoid crossing my path and potentially making me another late fellow.

"Yeah," I replied, nodding to the bear's Frisbee-sized pile. "First I want to study field butchering, orienteering, tracking, and most of all, firearm safety. And I'm not even really hungry right now." I still had a pound and a half of turkey jerky coursing through my system.

I lowered the gun, flipped the safety on, removed the shell, and quickly moved on, because I didn't want to dwell on my last-minute clumsiness being responsible for this hare's survival. Plenty of lightning bolts and skiddy ice patches had done the same for me. And I thought I knew right then that I would do it, eventually. Step Two, I mean. I felt I understood what it took to gather food, and it was good.

After a few minutes, I sat down and waited for Bob to catch up by making notes rationalizing how my laser printer fit into a subsistence life. I didn't tell him about this second shot not heard 'round the forest. Instead I whistled for Sunny, and didn't tell her about the bear's message either. The bear in my mind was by now wearing the fellow's hat and carrying his gun. We had plenty of time for food-gathering progress. I had learned just how much there was to this Step, and no one had gotten hurt. In Cheechako terms, that's a triumphant day.

* * * * *

The three of us peaked high above a second lake, and then turned around, having traveled seven waterfalls past the one toward which we had planned to bushwhack. We tiptoed aside to avoid sploshing in another new pile of bear scat as we began the long descent toward camp. Nobody spoke for more than an hour.

Finally, lazily, we found ourselves back at a switchback about half a mile above Odie's Lake. The forest was giving off an unfamiliar sense of proportion, as though we had shrunk. I felt like Alice. I could swear the bluebells were fuller, the roses further abloom than they had been when we hiked in. This is how Alaska works on body and mind: keeping an eye on the seasons here is somewhere between watching a minute hand and watching a second hand. If you pay attention you can see them change (visible plant growth over the course of a day is not unusual; visible philosophical change in a *Homo sapiens* only slightly less common).

Bob headed home and Sunny and I camped one more night in the meadow. Hiking back to the car in the morning, I had the nagging feeling that pre-bureaucratic humans didn't have to go through an internal debate to reach their Step Two conclusions. Bob and I had spent an awful lot of time talking about evolution on our expedition. In all the extra thought required for something as basic as food, I felt a sense of the less-discussed devolution.

"Well," I thought several times in the days after my hunting debut.

The Shots Not Heard 'round the Forest

"I can live with the internal debate. I'll look at it as a tradeoff for e-mail."

As soon as I got home (first I guiltily stopped for an Odie's turkey sandwich, where I confirmed that it was indeed Saturday), I called up my friend Marcus, who grew up hunting in the North Carolina hills. He gave me several suggestions for marksmanship drills. Two weeks later I went out to a deserted beach for my first target shooting exercise. The gun pushed back on my shoulder like a seatbelt on a very short stop and scared the heck out of Sunny, but it didn't explode.

I didn't really hit too many of the targets either, but I wasn't discouraged. I arguably would have hit that second snowshoe hare. I recognized my mind-set that afternoon on the beach as the same one with which I had bolstered myself in Hamilton's Cafe Lounge fourteen days earlier. As I packed up my smoking shotgun, I heard myself still saying, "You gotta start somewhere."

Step Three: Shelter

And that didn't arouse suspicion?

—Network newscaster, to on-site reporter at the cabin of the just-arrested Unabomber suspect, when told the suspect built his own home and lived without running water.

Chapter 9
Gory Drywalling

*L*aura hadn't mentioned it, but near the end of my second summer I realized that there was a Third Step with which I would eventually have to familiarize myself if I really wanted to Know How to Do Things. In retrospect, it's obvious: after warmth and food, one must have some sort of permanent shelter. If one wants to survive an Alaskan winter, at least.

My own cabin was…convertible to the point that I could tell wind direction by watching the door. I stuffed toilet paper in the most obvious gaps in its workmanship and still spent the winter waking up with ice in my water bottle. At times I would put sensitive electronic equipment in the fridge to warm it up.

Since this book is intended to document one year of my Alaskan foray, I must in the name of honesty disclose that I was not very far into this third and most cerebellum-demanding step by the time the chainsaw repair anniversary approached. In fact, Step Three is still a sticking point in my emergence from Cheechakohood several years later: it's not as easy to build a house as those who can do it insist.

I had no Step Three experience at all as of 1999. But I was tossed into it late in the summer, when my neighbor Shawna's house burned to the size of a potato chip. I would've seen the flames if I had been home when it happened, since she lived maybe a quarter mile down East End Road, between my cabin and Bob's.

I was out trying to explode tin cans with extreme prejudice when the neighborhood rebuilding effort got in full swing. Thus I got a brief but intense introduction to home building just within the parameters of my first Cheechako year. I ran into Shawna on my way home from my exercise in modern subsistence practice, my shotgun still warm.

Clearly having not conferred closely with Laura at the General Store, Shawna told me that "another two hands would always be appreciated," when I asked if there was anything I could do to help.

That wasn't the answer I really expected, I realized only at that moment. Her words suddenly reminded me that I was incapable of constructing so much as a mailbox post. It was the third dimension that tended to trip me up with three-dimensional structures. With flat-ish tasks like sanding and vacuuming, I was usually okay.

I sighed, Free Ranged my enthusiasm, and told Shawna I'd see her in the morning. With that exchange, I came to believe that Alaska would force its lessons on me, whether I was ready or not.

It was my second August in Fritz Creek. My once-proud, trans-Alaska woodpile was down to the dregs. The summer had peaked and the first chill winds were dropping their leafy teasers about what was next. In my blood, I felt that I was starting to understand the concept of cycles.

Surrounded by the first berries, I biked (and Sunny jogged) at around 10 the next morning to the charred rebuilding site for Shawna and her family. I did this with a good attitude, despite a nagging concern that my presence might result in a worsening of her housing situation.

Here's why: Shawna, a short-haired powerhouse of a thirty-something good-vibe factory, was of the yee-hawing, backslapping school of Mountain Womanhood, and her enthusiasm was infectious. I don't think I ever heard her speak below sixty avalanche-inducing decibels, even when she was telling me about most of her possessions going up in flames.

With her I was feeling that "help the fellow primate" dynamic I had always heard about in documentaries about the Amish and had experienced on the receiving end in various Roger Longhenry interactions. It felt nice to be giving back. I was deeply committed to self-congratulation that morning as I wheeled up my dirt street.

Gory Drywalling

"I am a good, nearly indigenous person," I told myself, even though some neighbors had been working on the house every day, for weeks.

It took about twenty seconds of hard pedaling before I could see Shawna's beams poking through the trees between our two streets. The place was starting to look like a home again already. Hopping off my bike in the tool-littered driveway, I noticed that outside the skeletal frame, the most congenitally Mountain Manly neighbors were helping Shawna's husband and stepson hand-mill the timber for the roof. From local spruce, no less. Inside, if you could call it that at this stage, it was evidently drywalling and plumbing week, I saw, when I from force of habit stepped through the part of the air that would one day be the front door.

* * * * *

Everyone else at the job site had the body language of having been working for a while already, like perhaps thirty years. A be-tattooed man who had been introduced to me as a recent ex-con (I thought as a joke), and who was staying with my oil man neighbor Dave, handed me some coffee and made friendly comments about my Tilley hat. Pipes, U-shaped tubing, and stacks of drywall flats lay about on the dirt floor.

I tripped over one of the last almost immediately, nearly piling on top of Gene McBride, the old homesteader. He was crouched like an inmate within the first floor bathroom's wall beams, marking with a pencil a place to cut a sheet of drywall for the east-facing wall.

"Howdy," I said with respect to Gene, who was the elder of this rural nook of Fritz Creek. He didn't know me well, but Gene'd always greeted me kindly when he saw me, usually considering my options while stuck in some ice ditch or mud bog. It must've been weird to see all these new people in Tilley hats and Vasque boots living on the land you staked out half a century earlier. But Gene took it well.

"Grrr," he growled at me in Old School Mountain Manese, not

looking up from his freehand straight line. This meant, "Hello, son. Nice to see you here, helping out your neighbor. Don't worry about that coffee you just spilled down my back."

Above our roofless heads clouds were moving in pearly fractals across the Fritz Creek sky. A perfect late summer day was peaking. Someone helped me up. Someone else pressed an Exacto knife and a tape measure into my palm, and I sort of leaped right in, trying to measure where we'd have to leave a hole in the drywall for a light fixture in the kitchen.

Gene, who can safely be described as grizzled, was running the operation. Covered in sawdust dandruff and encircled by a hula hoop of hanging protractors and power tools, he finished the drywall measurement he was working on. Then he watched me work with the tape measure for a few seconds. Then he informed me that my main job this day was to push in the center of drywall sheets with a two-by-four T-square. This was so that others around me could nail the big rectangles to the house's skeleton without any drooping in the middle.

Gene punctuated this directive by violently working the antenna of a nearby radio to more clearly project the offerings of his oldies station, while mumbling about all this bullshit "code" they didn't have in his day. I think he meant building safety code. In his day they didn't have a paved East End Road, either. Or a tow truck service in Homer. Or an outdoor gear co-op in Anchorage. It was all making me nostalgic for his day.

"What will I be nostalgic about at seventy?" I wondered. "All the forests and wolves in my day?"

Two hours later I was still pressing drywall, now into Shawna's once and future kitchen ceiling. Dave, Gene, and the ex-con nailed the pieces into the beams around me, and occasionally into their own fingers. That's evidently part of the process. Stretching upward from a stool, my limbs had been sprawled at almost jumping jack angles for at least an hour too long. I was starting to feel like a much, much weaker

Gory Drywalling

Atlas. That was my first Step Three job: standing very still. I appreciated the opportunity to watch Mountain Men work without revealing my various skill gaps. And I was apparently fairly good at it: no one had any criticisms of my performance as drywall presser. In fact, no one said anything at all to me as I stood very still. As a result, my mind was doing all the moving.

* * * * *

Since I have been thrust somewhat abruptly into the world of Step Three, I thought, this might be a good time for an assessment of my overall Cheechako-shedding progress over my first year and a half as an Alaskan.

Hmm. Well, if my Step One performance was a mixed bag (I shuddered simultaneously at what Mako thought of my slip outside his office and at about twenty-seven other temperature-related Cheechako incidents spread over the state), I had indisputably survived a winter. I felt that was pretty much key. Especially with another one clearly on its way. I believed surviving, all things considered, was far better than not surviving.

With regard to Step Two, well, I was still trying to blast holes in cans on the beach while bracing for the recoil. That didn't keep the freezer full. It'd be another couple of winters at least before I was serving indigenous stews. The moose and hare of the Kenai Peninsula were safe for a while.

As for this new Step Three busine . . . Here my assessment was delayed as I felt a powerful lap of wetness line my neck and face. I whipped my head around to identify its source. Tosha, Shawna's daughter and owner of the Sunny playmate Oreo the Rabbit, had snuck in through the empty kitchen window frame and was blasting me with some kind of semiautomatic water Uzi. Her firing posture was better than mine had been during that first gun lesson at Roger Longhenry's house.

For a few minutes I stood helpless on the stool, arms fully extended and glued to the T-square, getting soaked. My face quickly formed into a pleading expression I imagine Atlas never wore. It was a poor showing as either Earth- or drywall-supporter. Then I tried threatening Tosha that her next shot would be her last. That didn't seem to work on this braided Mountain Girl, and a mosquito was now feasting on my pinned hand. She thoughtfully blasted it off with a barrage that also knocked off my hat.

After chasing the eleven-year-old around the foundation for a while (and nearly decapitating Dave by abruptly releasing a piece of drywall on his head), I was able to return to the Step Three assessment at around 1:30 P.M.

What immediately struck me was the difficult-to-fathom observation that, despite my early spills and mismeasurements, the Fritz Creekers around the work site, particularly the recent ex-con, couldn't instantly tell I was embarking on my first day of home building.

"I think rough cut'll work just as well under the living room paneling," the ex-con said to me as to a colleague after we had positioned perhaps our ninetieth piece of drywall around this time. He holstered a hammer like it was a revolver.

"Oh, yeah, the wood knows what it wants to do," I heard myself replying in what, if I didn't know better, I might've described as a tone approaching Genuinely Relaxed. The ex-con seemed to completely accept that winged response.

This misperception on the part of my neighbors might simply have indicated that I had achieved journeyman status as a Free Range Bullshitter. For instance, after 540 days of primate-see, primate-do in Alaska, I could by now correctly pronounce "two-by-four" (you say it as one word: "toobuhfour"). And from the start of the workday at Shawna's, I noticed I was instinctively referring to every mechanical item as a female. I had even learned to pronounce "Hillary Clinton" as though it were an epithet. These are conventions not to be underestimated as milestones along the road to Mountain Manhood.

On the other hand, I did notice that I was by midafternoon a little bored with the repetitious process of drywall Atlas-ing. But that could just have been a result of the Bing Crosby marathon we had all been sentenced to on Gene's radio for more than four hours.

Overall, I could feel the idea of Step Three getting inside me. Since failing to bag a snowshoe hare, I had started having visions of an eventual home off the road system, or at least off the utility grid. I wanted to explore more remote parts of Alaska to pinpoint some pristine streamside spot that called out to Sunny and me as a homestead. The closer I got to another winter in my igloo-cabin, the more well-honed these visions were becoming. I just had thought the day when I would actually begin working toward this dream would be far, far in the future.

* * * * *

By the middle of the day at Shawna's, I realized that ideas had already been forming in my head about how I'd like my home to look. I had a whole list of characteristics, quirky and less so, in my fantasies. A treehouse fort with astronomical observatory didn't sound bad for a writing studio, for example. I like a bird's-eye view of things, in general, plus I would be on an even keel with the woodpeckers and hummingbirds, who are among my best friends. The fort would, of course, have a clear line of sight for my high-speed wireless Internet access.

In the main cabin an "arctic entry," that Alaskan phrase meaning "dirty place where you get undressed after a day in the mud/snow/ice/rain," might prevent my current mud-and-ash living room catastrophe. And, although it sounded "out there," even to me, I liked the idea of a spruce needle and moss living room carpet. It felt nice on my feet in the forest—why not at home? I'd even started imagining how I'd power this dream cabin (I'd been watching hydro and solar instructional videos).

In the years since leaving that first cabin, I have come to realize how fortunate I was to have both running water (even only seasonally) and grid electricity. Except for one house-sitting gig, I haven't had electricity since. I've used everything from solar to hydro to gas generator power, and once or twice I've been reduced to kerosene lanterns. Each passing year makes me realize that technology allows a totally functional modern home powered cleanly and without access to any grid. There's no need even to miss out on *Pink Panther* reruns.

Even back in Fritz Creek, I was already thinking in terms of "alternative" energy (my prediction is such sources won't be considered "alternative" for long). These visions were all promising Step Three signs, I thought, at Shawna's homesite. They reminded me of the desire to awaken that first carried me to Alaska. I felt that my life really was now intertwined with a place. In a sort of Step Three prequel, I was one impending fantasy away from picturing myself erecting (or helping erect) a terraced, multistoried structure that would actually stand. More than that, it would withstand a tsunami and a 10.4 earthquake.

Still, I remembered the Carburetor Pin Lesson of the pack ice as I drywalled. The Three Steps really represented about 13,223 skills that I was going to have to pick up just to maintain the more pleasant parts of my lifestyle that I didn't want to shed merely because I'd be living fifteen or twenty snowed-in miles from the nearest town. And this was before mastering that pesky third dimension in home building.

For example, if I moved off the grid, I'd probably have to get myself a pilot's license and a plane. Or if I lived by water, I'd need to maintain a powerful boat. I simply couldn't see giving up my fresh bagel and golf habits. And once or twice a year I might want to catch an off-Broadway play or eat at a sushi restaurant. Plus, people simply don't accept "avalanche" as an excuse for not turning up at their wedding in San Francisco.

Gory Drywalling

Probably most strongly grounding me in the awareness of my own Step Three Cheechakoness after a subarctic winter in a holy and holey cabin, was the deep respect I had come to give the concept of insulation. On a cellular level, I had literally evolved to learn that warm is better than cold. I made a note to mention this to Bob.

An insulated structure doesn't build itself. I knew this. That might've been the big message of the day at Shawna's. After just one day actually working on a house, I was launching apologies at every math teacher to whom I had ever whined "When will I ever use these formulas?" It took me about fifteen minutes of building to realize how much arithmetic is involved in airtight architecture.

But at least I wanted to learn. As I further became a drywall dust snowman under the flying hammers of my neighbors, I made a mental note to study the logarithmic tables. And I felt a surging sensation of being on the right track when I remembered that I had already booked my first flying lesson.

* * * * *

Unfortunately, immediately after the issuance of this relatively satisfactory Cheechako progress report, at around 1:40 P.M. everything started to fall apart at the job site. It was a simple case of How Good We All Had It a Moment Ago Syndrome, I tried to cheerfully explain to everyone later, when the blood had been cleaned up.

It started when, behind me, I heard a shrill scream of terror. The recent ex-con had nearly removed his left ring finger with an Exacto knife, while trying to unseal the titanium staples from our last crate of drywall sheets. I had noticed earlier that the manufacturer found it necessary to fuse its boxes as though they contained top secret weaponry.

When I spun around, the ex-con was emitting anatomical adjectives and prancing about in what seemed a most un-Mountain Manly manner. Streams of platelets spurted in a scarlet fountain with every beat of his heart. As he danced, he stared in awe at the realty of his life force flowing out of him at seventy beats a minute. So did I, in truth. I hated to think it, but it reminded me of the bowhead's butchering. "Wow," I thought objectively as gore flew like Old Faithful. "Step Three can be dangerous."

At about the moment my mind processed the fact that we had a genuine emergency on our hands (the ex-con really only had about nine and a half fingers at the moment), I heard a vague, metal-scrunching sound outside that I didn't feel good about at all. I next recall three things happening in almost chain reaction succession.

First, in an attempt to come to the ex-con's aid, I relinquished the role of Atlas (again nearly flattening Dave with a drywall blow to the head).

Second, I ran outside while shouting over my shoulder, "Don't worry! I've got some iodine at my cabin—keep pressure on that artery."

And third, I found Gene, who had been pulling out of the driveway in order to pick up a new batch of drywall in town, in the midst of yelling at Tosha for leaving her bicycle out of sight against the back bumper of his truck. Only it was my bicycle. And it was now roughly in the shape of a Mr. Twisty pretzel.

Tosha, who was facing back toward the work site, looked at me out of the corner of her eye but didn't rat me out. I stopped in my tracks to let the homesteader pull out in a ticked-off cloud of dust, unaware of the gory scene transpiring nine feet away.

* * * * *

Back inside the skeletal house, I heard Dave frantically chanting, "Call 911! Call 911!" There were no phones.

"No cops!" the ex-con yelled cryptically as he danced around in a "So I'm Going to Die" samba. In the background I could hear Bing singing, "Have Yourself a Merry Little Christmas."

"How recent an 'ex'-con?" I wondered, as I stupidly righted my

Gory Drywalling

knotted bike and tried to ride it home to get what might be the most well-used first aid kit in Southcentral Alaska. After three pedals I realized I was just going around in circles.

Still, I half-carried, half-wheeled the crippled frame alongside me so that it wouldn't be around when Gene returned. In terms of pain during travel, this was a decision that ranked up there with setting off alone across polar bear territory on a defective snowmachine.

Barely had I reached East End Road, Sunny at my heels, when I knocked my ankle savagely on a jagged pedal. This resulted in an agony-filled skip-hop that had me tripping over a protruding spoke and performing deep tissue acupuncture on my thigh as I collapsed to the ground in a pile of nettles.

That was when Laura drove by in her light blue pickup truck, slowing only to stick her head out the window and inquire of my writhing form, "Survive much?" You think she'd know the answer to that question by now. She beeped twice and continued up East End Road. Her carburetor appeared to be functioning fine.

I waved weakly from a prone position. As she disappeared over the horizon, I saw the little orange siren atop Laura's former maintenance vehicle catching sunlight as though she were some sort of Cheechako enforcement ranger.

Chapter 10
Remedial Indigenousness

I get it," I thought definitively as I dusted myself off. After being surrounded at every moment for eighteen months by people who seemed to innately have the fluid spatial relations and indigenous skills necessary to survive as a human animal, I was having a revelation.

What was finally dawning on me was that I and my cerebellum would have to pursue the Three Steps in Alaska the way a dyslexic reader works through a novel: slowly and surely, with the awareness that it will take a little more time than it does for the other folks. Remedial indigenousness, essentially. As I pulled nettles out of my skin, I held on to this new viewpoint with a firmness that convinced me I was no longer susceptible to hubris-inspired fantasies of pending Mountain Manhood or even general competence.

"A Roger Longhenry was born knowing to select PVC Number Whatever Pipe for a residential septic job," I reflected with que será acceptance. "I know how to find Macintosh-formatted double-density disks in Costco." When it came to the Three Steps, I had to recognize, I would be most successful pacing myself.

Fair enough. As usual, the lesson required some pain on my part. Both my ankle and thigh were dripping thin trails of blood. I hobbled home, still in the role of ad-hoc paramedic. I grabbed some bandages and disinfectant, and limped back to Shawna's. But by the time I arrived, the ex-con was already safely swathed in perhaps two hundred of Tosha's Flintstones Band-aides. I slapped a few of those on my own injuries, and then we all got back to Step Three. If anything, the bloodletting only reinvigorated us.

The workday wrapped up a few hours later, after I had helped connect my first toilet. I felt I had learned a lot for one day. For instance, I discovered that much of construction involves looking for missing parts. And I learned that when you're tired on a building site, you don't say, "I'm tired," you say, "I'm gonna grab a cup of coffee." There started to be an almost Barrow-amount of coffee breaks toward early evening.

But by the end of the day at Shawna's, I also genuinely had the first inkling that I might actually one distant day be at least partly responsible for my own shelter. I'd probably need an expert along to supervise, but in this realization I took comfort in the knowledge that even Alaska Natives traditionally divided the tasks. A Tlingit carver told me recently that the canoe builders tended to live along the British Columbia coast, while his people specialized in rendering fish oil. They'd trade it for finished boats. This dynamic for some reason comforted me.

* * * * *

We all helped mop up sawdust and gore from where Shawna's living room carpet will be. Most of the neighbors started to disperse at 5:00 PM Shawna and I hung out for a while, analyzing wallpaper patterns. I noticed that Grewingk Glacier, the ice mass that feeds the magic turquoise pond, had started sending its pulsar rhythm across the entire Kachemak Bay mind-set as I again made my way home at around 5:45. I was on foot, my by-default most reliable method of travel.

When its mist blanket lifted like this, the glacier tended to mesmerize me. A swirling aqua ice trail near the moraine formed the infinity symbol I seem to see embedded in practically everything in Alaska. My eyes circled around and around the reclining figure eight. It reminded me, as it always does, that one sun-soldered face on one of those peaks across the bay represented more now, more ideas, more space, more dimensions, more downright perspective than I could ever hope to explore in a lifetime. This vista was a humility mural. An infinitesimality lesson. Every shadow, every angle of reflected light, every time of day and change of season was a new look at life. I couldn't help but see things from many different viewpoints.

As I limped cabinward, I was elevated into the same full-body bliss that Sunny and I had felt when we saw our first rainbow off the cabin deck. Two summers of staring across the same gorgeous Bay only intensified its messages. It was never the same view twice.

* * * * *

Which is all well and good. But if I'd learned one thing in my first year and a half, it was that part of getting mystical in rural Alaska involves physically surviving while you do it. There's pretty much no way to get around that one.

Especially, I thought, as Sunny and I made our way down the driveway, if you've chosen to emulate a Rugged Individualist lifestyle in a Wal-Mart era. I felt the late afternoon subarctic sun piercing my skin like photon acupuncture needles. Sunny greeted the latest moose in our trees. Two moms with twins had been hanging out for the last couple of days. I took a deep breath. With the cold weather on the way, I saw in the trees surrounding the moose all the wood there was to be chopped. I saw all the snow there would be to shovel. All the car maintenance there would be to do.

It occurred to me: when you're indigenous, even incompetently returning to indigenousness, life takes up a lot of your time. There are only Two or Three Steps, but they can become your world. They can leave very little time for old neuroses and phantom fears. Which is perhaps the point.

I remembered a fun afternoon during my first summer in the cabin. I was visiting with a friend who was building her home across the bay. After touring her unbelievable bayview structure, I asked her when she thought it would all be finished.

"Finished?" she asked, puzzled. "There's always something to fix."

Remedial Indigenousness

Indeed, it seems to me that perhaps the most crucial component of Doing Things is making Doing Things your moment-to-moment priority. You never read accounts of pioneers saying things like, "After dropping the kids off at soccer practice and faxing over the brief to the firm, I stalked and butchered a wild ram." The kids are out there helping you with the ram's intestines. Everybody focuses on the necessary tasks.

I could feel it happening already. The number of inputs in my life had been cut like social programs under a Republican budget plan. But I felt busier than ever. Whatever else you are, life is your occupation if you're trying to remember indigenousness. And much of the year it's not a part-time occupation. Although as I write this I realize I now know people who built their homes off the grid while holding down full-time jobs as teachers. Hmm. Maybe it was just I who needed to focus so exclusively on the not-dying thing.

For instance, as I sniffed the air late in my first Step Three day, my rejuvenating indigenousness told me that it was just about time to *huck* up the chainsaw again. I spoke to Sunny. "Yep (spitting imaginary chaw). Step One all over again. That's me. Always on top of the next survival task. Whatever Step is called for."

To whit, as soon as I stepped inside the cabin, about twenty minutes after leaving Shawna's and bashing my usual tibia on the usual deck step, my eye was lured like a magnet to my misshapen, pathetically snow-damaged ceiling.

Negligence in winter roof shoveling is a tough mistake to forget, when the effects are staring down at you, quite literally, every moment of every day. The warped ceiling was the first thing I saw every morning when I opened my eyes to the sounds of chickadees calling, *Cheeeeeechako.*

Pulsing with glacially infused energy, I had a sudden and violent problem with the condition of my ceiling. It made me feel like part of my life had warped. So much for the momentary bout of patience that Laura in her truck had inspired.

As I examined the drooping bubble of misshapen tile above my mussed-up bed that evening, I pointed out to myself, "Now here is a contradiction. I expect to throw up a remote cabin, live off the materials around me, far off the road system, and all that. Shouldn't I first be able to maintain my rented cabin a mere eleven miles from the nearest home supply store?"

It was a cogent question of almost Laura-esque logic. It suddenly dawned on me that my roof negligence wasn't just a Step One issue or a Step Three issue. It was a focusing-on-indigenousness issue. There would be no Roger Longhenry to call when I lived off the grid. I shivered with premonitory fear at this realization.

The first fallen cottonwood leaves started dancing in prophetic wind tunnels on the deck as I stood frozen in trance for several minutes near my stove. I had a sequence of visions featuring my lonely, remote death caused by everything from choking to backfiring. And then I suddenly burst forth with a renewed Step Three vigor.

How do I know this? Within seconds, I had popped in a Morcheeba CD and found myself standing on my rickety canvas chair in the middle of the cabin, clutching a loose-handled hammer. I was underneath the mushy, flaking ceiling tiles most affrontedly shaken loose by the winter's weight.

"This is how quickly the big steps out of Cheechakohood can come," I was already gloating to myself as I fought to maintain my footing in the sagging-ass part of the chair. "In sudden leaps, like evolutionary mutations."

Ceiling repair work, I knew from watching the guys at Shawna's, is a complicated procedure requiring roof scaling and beams finding. But I felt I could visualize the entire job beforehand, as though I were a sudden inheritor of Roger Longhenry's spatial relations.

Remedial Indigenousness

Completely forgetting Laura's latest humility lesson, I was back in full fantasy mode, one of my favorite places to be. Today I would nail in the sagging tiles. Tomorrow I would head into town for some roof-repair shingles and sealant goop. I'd scramble on top of my home and remedy the mistakes of the winter, which were never to be repeated. By the following week I'd have my Polysorbate-free smokehouse built, and have Bob over for a sin-free indigenous meal.

Solid enough sentiments. But just as I was getting started, three nails jutting at odd angles from between my lips, my thumb exposed well within a radius likely to cause a fair barrage of colorful adjectives, I heard a knock on the bay window.

Dangerously off-balance though I was, I saw it was Tosha. And her mouth was flashing me the little O.

* * * * *

"My mom just wanted to make sure you were OK," she called from the deck.

I gave her the thumbs up.

"Well, I gotta go home to supper now," she said, and left.

Supper? I had no idea if it was 6:00 P.M. or 10:00 P.M. I just knew it was summer. And I was happy. I had just realized that I no longer thought Homer O'clock was a disease. I thought, and still think, it is a cure. I didn't come up here to Alaska to become an expert in the Two or Three Steps. I came here to be here.

A kiss of glacial breeze washed over me through the redundantly open cabin door. On the other side of the bay window my sweaty work shirt was flapping on the deck railing. The fireweed were bursting like organic ordnance and poking through the deck, where my dog was working on a bone. The breeze was giving her a punk look.

It was almost exactly one year after some primeval part of me awakened and started me thinking it was high time to get a woodstove into this cabin before winter hit. As yet another August wound down, I still could not really Do the Indigenous Things. But I knew what they were. And, more importantly, I thought I might be starting to know who I was.

Aarigaa.

Epilogue

We're a couple more wars in now, and there have been some changes in my life since 1999.

JM and I didn't work out as a couple. I think I'll keep the details between us. I learned so much from her and appreciate our time together more than I can say. She was deadpan but never unkind in her observations of my Cheechako behavior. It's tough to forget a person who accompanied you during such a happy time in your life.

Mako still runs a great water-taxi service out of Homer.

The last e-mail I got from Roger was from Minnesota. Still no mention of the cathedral job. Don't be surprised if it happens, though. Remember, Free Ranging almost always contains the truth.

The Leavitts are doing well and still eating *muktuk.*

Bob moved home to Seattle, where he works on environmental issues.

The last time I saw Laura was almost three years ago, when I stopped into the Fritz Creek General Store on a visit to the Homer area. She seemed surprised when I told her she was mentioned in a book I was writing.

Sunny skied with me a week before she died, two years ago, of lung cancer.

Driving While Happy is still not illegal in Alaska.

Me, I'm still here in the Last Frontier. I live in a more manually navigable portion of coastal Alaska now. So I do a lot of kayaking and crabbing and stuff.

I have probably made the most progress when it comes to Step Two. Four years after the seminal experiences on the pack ice and in the forest with the disappearing hare, I have become a functional, if not an adept, fisherman. From my new home in Southeast Alaska, I catch my fifty salmon per summer, which gets me through the winter with sufficient protein.

I believe the sense of natural rightness in gathering the local food source, which I witnessed in my time with the Leavitts and discussed so intensely with Bob, solidified my Step Two resolve. I still haven't hunted a moose, though I have read books featuring macabre diagrams about how to butcher one. I don't relish the idea, but I'll probably do it. I think it's healthier than buying even lovingly crafted turkey sandwiches.

As of this writing, the poles still haven't reversed.

I have largely lived off the grid for the past three years. Lately I have been considering living part of the year in a desert wilderness ecosystem. It's hard to choose between this and Alaska: I love them both and so might live in both. But I might just be writing this because winter is coming and I'm already cold. Last winter was terrible: the pollution-free hydropower generator at the house I was renting died midway through the winter and I had no wood ready as backup. Though it was a pretty warm winter, I'd leave my bagels outside to stay frozen overnight and the ravens would devour them by morning.

Still, the values instilled in me during my first year as a rural human have solidified. I can say with some confidence that I will never live in a big city again. It's too beautiful here on Planet Earth. And I believe open space, clean water, and noise and light pollution issues are among the most important our species face: they are tied into everything else, including more important sounding phrases like "world hunger," "overpopulation," "strong economy," and "war and peace."

We are at a time in history where there is no way to know what skills or training are necessary to thrive in the near future. So I'm going basic. Whether we face a societal crash or the discovery of an interplanetary wormhole, I figure we all have to eat. And stay warm. And have shelter. Three Steps.

I am still working on all of the skills I danced around during the events recounted in this book. I am a master of none, although I am better at The Walk. My back is glad for this. But my antics continue to provide humor for many people who don't have televisions. I might not exactly be a Cheechako anymore, but I am still Not Really an Alaskan Mountain Man. It sure is fun trying. I am always pushing myself in some way. I might be madly paddling in a kayak to outrun a scary frontal system, or I might be trying to string some sophisticated chickenwire fencing so a porcupine can't get into my peas.

"That's what all of this really is about, this haphazard pursuit of an elusive Mountain Manhood," I thought the other day. "With nearly constant change perpetually unfolding in front of me, I might continually be open to growth—I might shut up and listen to whatever life wants me to do."

Parts of this journey had been hard, even scarring, I realize with a pang. And I know there will be more pain to come—that's what happens when one is truly open to experience. But the room for growth has been worth the scars. It massages genes not previously exercised. It allows even a shaggy-haired Cheechako to live a good portion of his life flush against the mystical, whose hints in the sound of raven wings once merely sounded like pretty noise.